Other Books by Hesketh Pearson
CONAN DOYLE
A LIFE OF SHAKESPEARE
A SEAL FLIES BY

DOCTOR DARWIN

From the portrait by J. Wright in the National Portrait Gallery

ERASMUS DARWIN

DOCTOR DARWIN

BY

HESKETH PEARSON

"Dr. Krause is justified in saying of
Erasmus Darwin 'that he was the first
who proposed and persistently carried out
a well - rounded theory' of evolution."

Samuel Butler.

Walker and Company
New York

TO
MY MOTHER

Published simultaneously in Canada by George J. McLeod, Limited, Toronto.

Library of Congress Catalog Card Number: 63-19203

Printed in the United States of America from type set in Great Britain.

PREFACE

It is, perhaps, as the man who gave a creed to Creative Evolution that Dr. Erasmus Darwin chiefly interests us to-day. But his claims to our attention are far wider than that. He was the grandfather of Charles Darwin by his first marriage, and of Sir Francis Galton by his second. There is hardly an idea and hardly an invention in the world of to-day that he did not father or foresee, from the philosophy of Mr. Bernard Shaw to the phonograph of Mr. Thomas Edison, from eugenics and evolution to aeroplanes and submarines, from psycho-analysis to antiseptics. He founded the Lunar Society—the most remarkable group of thinkers and inventors in the eighteenth century—which had a more potent effect upon civilization than that of any other society in history. He was the greatest philosopher and physician of his day, and a poet who won the unstinted praise of Cowper and Walpole. He was a notable humanitarian and reformer, centuries ahead of his time, and, rarer still, an extremely benevolent and reasonable human being. Naturally these virtues were balanced by vices, perhaps the worst being his strong aversion to "spirituous potation."

The majority of reliable biographies are unreadable, and the majority of readable biographies are unreliable. As this is the first full-length biography of the parent of Creative Evolution, I have done my best to combine authority with interest. Some of my readers may think that I have devoted too much space to the doctor's friends. But to know a man well one must know his friends ; indeed, a man's friendships tell us far more about him than his love-affairs. No one has so far attempted a description of the Lunar Society and its leading members. I have tried to make up for this serious deficiency in biographical literature. Three of the members—Erasmus Darwin, James Keir, and Samuel Galton—were my great- (three times) grandfathers, which accounts for the fact that I have had access to unpublished material. This is acknowledged in the bibliography at the end of the book.

Pilgrims to Lichfield, the home of Dr. Darwin for twenty-five years, will observe with pleasure a large signpost in the main street. Hurrying towards it they will read these words : " To the Statue of King Edward VII." Is it too much to hope that, some day, there will be another statue (and perhaps even another signpost) to the physician, philosopher, and poet whose thoughts live on in the works of other men ?

H. P.

1930.

CONTENTS

DOCTOR DARWIN

CHAPTER I

THE EARLY EVOLUTIONIST

ERASMUS DARWIN was born on 12 December, 1731, at Elston Hall, in the county of Nottingham. His father was of a studious nature, more interested in fossils than in sport. His mother, if one can judge character from countenance, was strong-willed, energetic, and extremely capable. She was also something of a scholar ; but a short litany written by her husband seems to suggest that he had not married her for her familiarity with the classics :

> From a morning that doth shine,
> From a boy that drinketh wine,
> From a wife that talketh Latine,
> Good Lord deliver me.

As a child Erasmus experimented with poetry, clocks, and electricity, thus foreshadowing his later interests and achievements. He also displayed a healthy dislike for exercise, field sports, and rural diversions, and his brothers could never get him to participate in their pastimes without a considerable amount of preliminary ragging.

At the age of ten he was sent to Chesterfield School, and remained there till he was nineteen. He liked his masters at school, and they seem to have encouraged him in his poetic exercises. A letter he wrote to his sister while at Chesterfield has been preserved. She sent him a record of her abstinence for the first five days of Lent, and asked for an account of his own, adding : "As soon as we kill our hog I intend to take part thereof with ye Family, for I'm informed by a Learned Divine y^t Hogs Flesh is Fish, and has been so ever since ye Devil entered into y^m and they ran into ye sea ; if you and the rest of the Casuists in your neighbourhood are of ye same oppinion, it will be a greater satisfaction to me, in resolving so knotty a point of Conscience."

Erasmus, aged sixteen, replied as follows :

Dear Sister,

I received yours about a fortnight after ye date y^t I must begg to be excused for not answering it sooner: besides I have some substantial Reasons, as having a mind to see Lent almost expired, before I would vouch for my Abstinence throughout ye whole: and not having had a convenient opportunity to consult a Synod of my learned friends about your ingenious Conscience, and I must inform you we unanimously agree in ye Opinion of ye Learned Divine you mention, that Swine may indeed be fish but then they are a devilish sort of fish; and we can prove from ye same Authority that all fish is flesh whence we affirm Porck not only to be flesh but a devilish sort of flesh; and I would advise you for Conscience sake altogether to abstain from tasting it; as I can assure you I have done, tho' roast Pork has come to Table several Times; and for my own part have lived upon Puding, milk, and vegetables all this Lent; but don't mistake me, I don't mean I have not touch'd roast beef, mutton, veal, goose, fowl, &c. for what are all these ? All flesh is grass! Was I to give you a journal of a Week, it would be stuft so full of Greek and

Latin as translation verses, themes, annotation Exercises and ye like, it would not only be very tedious and insipid but perfectly unintelligible to any but Schoolboys.

I fancy you forgot in Yours to inform me y^t your Cheek was quite settled by your Temperance, but however I can easily suppose it. For ye temperate enjoy an ever-blooming Health free from all ye Infections and disorders luxurious mortals are subject to, the whimsical Tribe of Phisitians cheated of their fees may sit down in penury and Want, they may curse mankind and imprecate the Gods and call down y^t parent of all Diseases, luxury, to infest Mankind, luxury more distructive than ye Sharpest Famine; tho' all the Distempers that ever Satan inflicted upon Job hover over ye intemperate; they would play harmless round our Heads, nor dare to touch a single Hair. We should not meet those pale thin and haggard countenances which every day present themselves to us. No doubt men would still live their Hunderd, and Methusalem would lose his Character; fever banished from our Streets, limping Gout would fly ye land, and Sedentary Stone would vanish into oblivion and death himself be slain.

I could for ever rail against Luxury, and for ever panegyrize upon abstinence, had I not already encroach'd too far upon your Patience, but it being Lent the exercise of y^t Christian virtue may not be amiss, so I shall proceed a little furder. . . .

[What follows is illegible, except the last line.]

P.S.—Excuse Hast, supper being called, very Hungry.

In 1750 Erasmus and his two elder brothers went to St. John's College, Cambridge. This put a severe strain on their father's income, and they had to be economical to the point of discomfort. Many years later he told his wife that if she cut the heel out of a stocking he could put a new one in without missing a stitch, as he had had to mend his own clothes while at Cambridge.

He won a scholarship at John's (£16 a year), studied the classics, mathematics, and medicine, took his B.A. degree, and wrote a lot of poetry. One of his poems, on *The Death of Prince Frederick*, was published forty-four years later in the *European Magazine*. It cannot truthfully be said that the world is the poorer because the others were not published.

In 1754 he went to Edinburgh, where he continued his study of medicine and his practice of economy. There is among the papers in his Commonplace Book a slip bearing these words : " Nov. 26, 1854. Reciev'd of E. Darwin the sum of six pounds twelve shillings for his Board from July 13 to Oct. 13. Margt. Ogston (Edinbro)." Even his sister would have approved such Lenten living.

At Edinburgh he founded a lifelong friendship with James Keir, afterwards a famous chemist. It is probable that their friendship, more than any other single factor, was responsible for the formation in later years of the celebrated Lunar Society. Unfortunately Darwin's intimate friends were not Boswells. The most valuable material for a personal portrait of him was inspired partly by the hatred of one woman, and partly by the vanity of another. His friends, aided and abetted by himself, were more interested in ideas than in idiosyncrasies. Thus Keir, when asked for personal details of Erasmus's Edinburgh days, could only supply the following : " The classical and literary attainments which he had acquired at Cambridge gave him, when he came to Edinburgh, together with his poetical talents and ready wit, a distinguished superiority among the students there."

Not even a modern biographer could deduce from this that Keir and Darwin had " heard the chimes at midnight." Happily another friend, while carefully preserving his anonymity, has left it on record that " in his youth Dr. Darwin was fond of sacrificing to both Bacchus and Venus ; but he soon discovered that he could not continue his devotions to both these deities without destroying his health and constitution. He therefore resolved to relinquish Bacchus, but his affection for Venus was retained to the last period of life."

One letter has come down to us from his Edinburgh days. It was written in 1754, when he was twenty-three, and proves that he was an evolutionist a generation before the appearance of *The Botanic Garden*. It was addressed to Dr. Okes, of Exeter :

Yesterday's post brought me the disagreeable news of my father's departure out of this sinful world.

He was a man of more sense than learning; of very great industry in the law, even after he had no business, nor expectation of any. He was frugal, but not covetous; very tender to his children, but still kept them at an awful kind of distance. He passed through this life with honesty and industry, and brought up seven healthy children to follow his example.

He was 72 years old, and died the 20th of this current November 1754. "Blessed are they that die in the Lord."

That there exists a superior *ens entium*, which formed these wonderful creatures, is a mathematical demonstration. That He influences things by a particular providence, is not so evident. The probability, according to my notion, is against it, since general laws seem sufficient for that end. Shall we say no particular providence is necessary to roll this Planet round the Sun, and yet affirm it necessary in turning up *cinque* and *quatorze*, while shaking a box of dice or giving each his daily bread? The light of Nature affords us not a single argument for a future state; this is the only one, that it is possible with God, since He who made us out of nothing can surely re-create us; and that He will do this is what we humbly hope. . . .

Darwin went to Cambridge in 1755 to take his Bachelor of Medicine degree, returned to Edinburgh, and then started practice as a physician in Nottingham in the autumn of 1756. He would have commenced his career in London if only he could have obtained some immediate patronage. But one had to wait for patients in London.

Nottingham was quite a different proposition. He was known, his family was known, in the county, and he could afford to wait for patients. But either the inhabitants of Nottingham did not associate the name of Darwin with drugs, or they were satisfied with the doctors they already had. The fact remains that patients were few and far between, and after eight weeks he found he could not wait for them any longer.

While in Nottingham, however, he was not idle. He composed poetry, wrote a batch of Latin letters to an Edinburgh friend—son of the German philosopher Reimarus—who had just taken his degree at Leyden, speculated upon the action of the human soul, compared it with electricity, and interested himself in shorthand.

He also took a keen personal interest in the welfare

of a young working-man, who he sent to a London surgeon for a serious operation. Apparently he thought that the surgeon's fee of six guineas was excessive, since the patient was " a poor young man " who had nothing " but what hard labour gives him." He therefore helped the victim out of his own pocket, and sent an anonymous letter to the surgeon telling him exactly what he thought of him. When accused of having written the letter he refused to own up, but declared that he was " glad there are Persons who will revenge Faults the Law can not take hold of."

Eventually the surgeon returned four guineas to his patient, and Dr. Darwin carried his empty purse and his full heart to Lichfield.

CHAPTER II

LICHFIELD AND LOVE

HE arrived at Lichfield with letters of introduction to Canon Seward and Lady Gresley. The house of the former was the chief social and intellectual centre of the place. The canon and his family lived in the bishop's palace in the cathedral close—the bishop preferring to live elsewhere. One of the canon's daughters, Anna Seward, is known to fame as "The Swan of Lichfield." After his death she wrote a book about Dr. Darwin, on which a biographer must draw pretty extensively. We shall therefore meet her at frequent intervals in the course of these pages. But when the doctor arrived at Lichfield in November, 1756, she was only nine years old.

Let us try to picture him as he stood on the threshold of his professional career. Rather above the medium height, his limbs were heavy and his body was unsymmetrical. Already, at the age of twenty-five, there were signs of corpulence, though he was healthy, strong, and extremely active. A severe attack of smallpox had left its traces on his face, about which there was little refinement. His gait was clumsy and he sometimes walked with his tongue hanging out of his mouth. He dressed carelessly, and the large full-bottomed wig he then wore made him look twice his

8

age. On entering a room or accosting his friends his smile, we are told, was winning and sunny, though the general expression of his features, when not animated by conversation, was " rather saturnine than sprightly."

He stammered excessively, but whatever he said, whether grave or gay, was well worth waiting for. The fact that Dr. Johnson did not care to wait was no doubt one of the reasons why they were always at daggers drawn. More solid reasons will appear later on. It is curious that Darwin never managed to cure himself of what, to a great talker, is a more serious handicap than a hare-lip. " There are two sorts of agreeable persons in conversation parties," he once said ; " agreeable talkers and agreeable listeners " — yet it is hardly agreeable to listen to the cacophonies and sibilations of a stutterer.

At a later date he attributed the habit to " a too great diffidence or bashfulness, joined with an ambition of shining in conversation." On the strength of that statement one wonders whether his own trick of speech was not carefully cultivated for conversational purposes. While he was stammering, perhaps, his wits were at work preparing his *bons mots*, which were greeted all the more heartily because of the relief his audience felt after a painful period of verbal parturition. A young man once asked him, in a possibly offensive manner, whether he didn't find stammering rather inconvenient. " No, sir," he replied, " it gives me time for reflection, and saves me from answering impertinent questions."

Nevertheless, ten years after his arrival at Lichfield, he sent his eldest son to France, in the hope that, if he was not allowed to speak English for a time, he would be cured of the same disease. The boy returned a year later, spoke French fluently for the rest of his life, but continued to stammer in English.

Dr. Darwin was not the only big talker of his time who suffered from this impediment. Dr. Caleb Hardinge, Physician to the Tower, was a terrific wind-bag, who had been utterly spoilt by half the duchesses of the day. He monopolized the conversation wherever he went, and was so popular that his insolence passed for wit. David Garrick brought him to Lich-field, and introduced him to Darwin. After they had made inharmonious sounds at one another for a minute or two, Hardinge, who wasn't used to being stam-mered down, burst forth with : " M-my dear d-doctor, you have a d-damned ugly t-trick of st-stuttering. I am s-sure I could c-cure you." To which Darwin rejoined: "Ph-physician, h-heal thyself!"

It has been necessary to labour this defect of Darwin's at the outset, because it makes his rapid rise to social and medical pre-eminence all the more remarkable.

Shortly after his arrival in Lichfield he made a sensation. A gentleman of some note in Staffordshire, named Mr. Inge, was dangerously ill. The leading doctor of the neighbourhood, after trying every experi-ment he could think of, at length pronounced the disease incurable, and told Mr. Inge to prepare for an early death. As it was now a case of kill or cure, the dying man's mother sent for the newly-arrived and untried Dr. Darwin, who, by an entirely novel course of treatment, cured him completely. Thus the young

physician's fame was spread abroad in the land. From
that moment he had no rival in Lichfield or its neighbourhood; and as his medical methods were henceforth
described by his professional competitors as rash,
dangerously experimental, and theoretic, we may be
sure that he cured his patients at a shamefully
unfashionable rate.

Erasmus had not been in Lichfield a year before he
fell in love with Miss Mary Howard, who lived with
her family in the cathedral close. Anna Seward
describes her as " a blooming and lovely young lady
of eighteen. A mind which had native strength ;
an awakened taste for the works of imagination ;
ingenuous sweetness ; delicacy animated by sprightliness, and sustained by fortitude, made her a capable
as well as fascinating companion even to a man of
talents so illustrious."

On 24 December, 1757, we find Erasmus writing
to her from Darlaston in this strain :

Dear Polly,

As I was turning over some old mouldy volumes, that were
laid upon a Shelf in a Closet of my Bed-chamber; one I found,
after blowing the Dust from it with a Pair of Bellows, to be a
Receipt Book, formerly, no doubt, belonging to some good
old Lady of the Family. The Title Page (so much of it as
the rats had left) told us it was "a Bouk off verry monny
muckle vallyed Receipts bouth in Kookery and Physicks."
Upon one Page was "To make Pye-Crust,"—in another
"To make Wall-Crust,"—"To make Tarts,"—and at length
"To make Love." "This Receipt," says I, "must be curious,
I'll send it to Miss Howard next Post, let the way of making
it be what it will."—Thus it is "To make Love. Take of

Sweet-William and of Rose-Mary, of each as much as is sufficient. To the former of these add of Honesty and Herb-of-grace; and to the latter of Eye-bright and Mother-wort of each a large handful: mix them separately, and then, chopping them altogether, add one Plumb, two sprigs of Heart's Ease and a little Tyme. And it makes a most excellent dish, probatum est. Some put in Rue, and Cuckold-Pint, and Heart-Chokes, and Coxcoms, and Violents; But these spoil the flavour of it entirely, and I even disprove of Sallery which some good Cooks order to be mix'd with it. I have frequently seen it toss'd up with all these at the Tables of the Great, where no Body would eat of it, the very appearance was so disagreeable."

Then followed "Another Receipt to make Love," which began: "Take two Sheep's Hearts, pierce them many times through with a Scewer to make them Tender, lay them upon a quick Fire, and then taking one Handful"—here Time with his long Teeth had gnattered away the remainder of this Leaf. At the Top of the next Page, begins "To make an honest Man." "This is no new dish to me," says I, "besides it is now quite old Fashioned; I won't read it." Then follow'd "To make a good Wife." "Pshaw," continued I, "an acquaintance of mine, a young Lady of Lichfield, knows how to make this Dish better than any other Person in the World, and she has promised to treat me with it sometime," and thus in a Pett threw doun the Book, and would not read any more at that Time. If I should open it again to-morrow, whatever curious and useful receipts I shall meet with, my dear Polly may expect an account of them in another Letter.

I have the Pleasure of your last Letter, am glad to hear thy cold is gone, but do not see why it should keep you from the concert, because it was gone. We drink your Health every day here, by the Name of Dulcinea del Toboso, and I told Mrs. Jervis and Miss Jervis that we were to have been married yesterday, about which they teased me all the Evening. I heard nothing of Miss Fletcher's Fever before. I will certainly be with Thee on Wednesday evening, the Writings are at my House, and may be dispatched that night, and if a License takes up any Time (for I know nothing at all about these Things) I should be glad if Mr. Howard would order one, and by this means, dear Polly, we may have the Ceremony over next morning at eight o'clock, before any Body in Lichfield can know almost of my being come Home. If a License is to be had the Day before, I could wish it may be put off till late in the Evening, as the Voice of Fame makes such quick Dispatch with any News in so small a Place as Lichfield. . . . I think this is much the best scheme, for to stay a few Days after my Return could serve no Purpose, it would only make us more watch'd and teazed by the Eye and Tongue of Impertinence. . . . I shall by this Post apprize my Sister to be ready, and have the House clean, and I wish you would give her Instructions about any trivial affairs, that I cannot recollect, such as a cake you mentioned, and tell her the Person of whom, and the Time when it must be made, &c. I'll desire her to wait upon you for this Purpose. Perhaps Miss Nelly White need not know the precise Time till the Night before, but this as you please, as I . . . [illegible] You could rely upon her Secrecy, and it's a Trifle, if any Body should know. Matrimony, my dear girl, is undoubtedly a serious affair, (if any Thing be such) because it is an affair for Life: But, as we have deliberately determin'd, do not let us be *frighted* about this Change of Life; or however, not let any breathing Creature perceive that we have either Fears or Pleasures upon this Occasion; as I am certainly convinced, that the best of Confidants (tho' experienced on a thousand other Occasions) could as easily hold a burning cinder in their Mouth as anything the least ridiculous about a new married couple! I have ordered the Writings to be sent to Mr. Howard that he may peruse and fill up the blanks at his Leizure, as it will (I foresee) be dark night before I get to ·Lichfield on Wednesday. Mrs. Jervis and Miss desire their Compl. to you, and often say how glad she shall be to see you

for a few Days at any Time.   I shall be glad, Polly, if thou
hast Time on Sunday night, if thou wilt favour me with a few
Lines by the return of the Post, to tell me how Thou doest,
&c.—My Compl. wait on Mr. Howard if He be returned. . . .
My sister will wait upon you, and I hope, Polly, Thou wilt
make no Scruple of giving her Orders about whatever you
chuse, or think necessary.   I told her Nelly White is to be
Bride-Maid.   Happiness attend Thee!   Adieu.

> from, my dear Girl,
> > thy sincere Friend,
> > > E. Darwin.

P.S.—Nothing about death in this Letter, Polly.

They were married four days later, and shortly after
the event Erasmus bought " an old half-timbered
house in the cathedral vicarage, adding a handsome new
front, with Venetian windows, and commodious apartments."   Let Miss Seward continue the description :
" This front looked towards Beacon Street, but had
no street annoyance, being separated from it by a
narrow, deep dingle, which, when the doctor purchased the premises, was overgrown with tangled briars
and knot-grass.   In ancient days it was the receptacle
of that water, which moated the close in a semicircle,
the other half being defended by the minster pool.
A fortunate opening, between the opposite houses and
this which has been described, gives it a prospect
sufficiently extensive, of pleasant and umbrageous fields.
Across the dell, between his house and the street,
Dr. Darwin flung a broad bridge of shallow steps with
Chinese paling, descending from his hall-door to the
pavement.   The tangled and hollow bottom he cleared
into lawny smoothness, and made a terrace on the bank,

which stretched in a line, level with the floor of his apartments, planting the steep declivity with lilacs and rose-bushes ; while he screened his terrace from the gaze of passengers, and the summer sun,

> By all that higher grew,
> Of firm and fragrant leaf.   Then swiftly rose
> Acanthus, and each odorous bushy shrub,
> To fence the verdant wall."

When Erasmus left Lichfield his house was purchased by a gentleman who destroyed the dell and substituted a circular coach-road from the street to the hall-door. Miss Seward did not regard the alteration as an improvement.

CHAPTER III

CHARACTER AND ANECDOTES

A CONTINUOUS narrative of the life of Dr. Darwin cannot be written. The materials are not available. A biographer can only portray him as he appeared on various occasions to different people. But in order that his personality may be impressed upon the reader at the outset, a number of anecdotes and character-sketches shall prelude the account of his activities and friendships.

" Conscious of great native elevation above the general standard of intellect," Miss Seward tells us, " he became, early in life, sore upon opposition, whether in argument or conduct, and always revenged it by sarcasm of very keen edge. Nor was he less impatient of the sallies of egotism and vanity, even when they were in so slight a degree, that strict politeness would rather tolerate than ridicule them. Dr. Darwin seldom failed to present their caricature in jocose but wounding irony."

Our chronicler gives us an instance of his " wounding irony." He was entertaining a number of people at his house when a lady and gentleman, unknown to him, were announced. The lady was tall, fat, ruddy, and blatant. The gentleman was small, meek, pale, self-effacing, and effeminate. The moment they entered the lady opened fire :

" Dr. Darwin, I seek you not as a physician, but as a *belle esprit*. I make this husband of mine"—and she glared at the mouse-like object at her side—" treat me every summer with a tour through one of the British counties, to explore whatever it contains worth the attention of ingenious people. On arriving at the several inns in our route I always search out the man of the vicinity most distinguished for his genius and taste, and introduce myself, that he may direct, as the objects of our examination, whatever is curious in nature, art, or science. Lichfield will be our head-quarters during several days. Come, doctor, whither must we go, what must we investigate to-morrow, and the next day, and the next? Here are my tablets and pencil."

Dr. Darwin was quite equal to the occasion. With the utmost politeness he stammered out: "You arrive, m-madam, at a fortunate juncture. T-to-morrow you will have an opportunity of surveying an annual exhibition p-perfectly w-worth your attention. T-to-morrow, m-madam, you will go to T-tutbury b-bull-running."

His remark was received by the company with a roar of merriment. The lady nearly burst with indignation. Her bosom heaved and her eyes flashed fury. Then, gathering her husband to her, she hissed forth : " I was recommended to a man of genius, and I find him insolent and ill-bred," and stormed out of the room. After her departure several of his guests wanted to know why the doctor had been so harsh.

" I chose," he said, " to avenge the cause of the little

man, whose nothingness was so ostentatiously displayed by his lady-wife. Her vanity has had a smart emetic. If it abates the symptoms, she will have reason to thank her physician, who administered without hope of a fee."

Dr. Darwin never found it difficult to be disagreeable in a good cause. A certain lady of rank married a widower, and became so jealous of his former wife that she cut and spoiled her picture, which was hanging in one of the rooms. The husband, thinking his wife was going mad, was greatly alarmed and sent for Dr. Darwin. When he arrived he told her in the plainest manner many unpleasant truths, amongst others that the former wife was infinitely her superior in every respect, including beauty. The lady was utterly cowed by this treatment, and Darwin advised her husband to hint that he should be sent for if ever again she gave him any trouble. The plan succeeded perfectly. For the remainder of their married life the barest mention of the doctor's name was quite sufficient to keep her in order.

The doctor was not a regular churchgoer, though the gentleman who related the following story was perhaps a little wide of the mark in attributing the doctor's abstinence from public prayers to his professional engagements. At any rate, he attended divine service in the cathedral when the new bishop, Hurd, preached his first sermon. Hurd was a classical scholar, and fancied himself as a rhetorician. He also believed he would make a good impression if he spoke well above the heads of his congregation. On this occasion everybody was enchanted by his flights of eloquence, and even Dr. Darwin, as he quitted the cathedral, appeared to be deeply impressed.

" Well, doctor, how did you like the bishop's discourse ? " asked a friend.

The doctor was taken by surprise and stuttered forth : " The bishop's discourse, sir ? . . . why . . . it . . . c-contained some v-very g-good w-words indeed, sir."

This was repeated to the bishop, who took it to heart, but never expressed his gratitude to the doctor.

Anna Seward is our sole authority for the report that Dr. Darwin and Dr. Johnson never got on well together ; but as she knew them both well, and as they belonged to two radically different schools of thought, we may accept her statement without reserve. This is what she says :

" Dr. Johnson was several times at Lichfield . . . while Dr. Darwin was one of its inhabitants. They had one or two interviews, but never afterwards sought each other. Mutual and strong dislike subsisted between them. . . . But Johnson liked only *worshippers* . . . it was an arduous hazard to the feelings of the company to oppose, in the slightest degree, Dr. Johnson's opinions. His stentor lungs ; that combination of wit, humour, and eloquence, which ' could make the worse appear the better reason ' ; that sarcastic contempt of his antagonist, never suppressed or even softened by the due restraints of good-breeding, were sufficient to close the lips, in his presence, of men who could have met him in fair argument, on *any* ground, literary or political, moral or characteristic. Where Dr. Johnson was, Dr. Darwin had no chance of being heard, though at least his equal in genius, his superior in science ; nor indeed, from his impeded utterance, in the company of *any* overbearing declaimer ; and he was too intellectually great to be an humble listener to Johnson, therefore he shunned him on having experienced what manner of man he was. The surly dictator felt the mortification, and revenged it, by *affecting* to avow his disdain of powers too distinguished to be an object of *genuine* scorn. Dr. Darwin, in his turn, was not much more just to Dr. Johnson's genius. He uniformly spoke of him in terms which, had they been deserved, would have justified Churchill's 'immane Pomposo,' as an appellation of *scorn*; since, if his person was huge, and his manners pompous and violent, so were his talents vast and powerful, in a degree from which only prejudice and resentment could withhold respect.''

On the other hand, Darwin once expressed the view that Johnson's line ''Slow rises worth, by poverty depressed'' was much superior to the original; while Johnson unconsciously paid Darwin a compliment when he praised Miss Seward's *Ode on the Death of Captain Cook*, all the best lines of which were written by Darwin.

Sir Walter Scott says: ''Neither Dr. Darwin nor Miss Seward were partial to the great moralist. There was, perhaps, some aristocratic prejudice in their dislike, for the despotic manners of Dr. Johnson were least likely to be tolerated where the lowness of his origin was in fresh recollection.''

This, however, only proves that Sir Walter could appreciate aristocratic prejudice more thoroughly than intellectual antipathy. Darwin was incapable of the former and criticized or praised people irrespective of the class to which they belonged. Indeed, he once wrote a verse in which he derisively coupled Anna's father with Johnson, as editors of Beaumont and Shakespeare respectively:

From Lichfield famed two giant critics come,
Tremble, ye Poets ! hear them ! " Fe, Fo, Fum ! "
By Seward's arm the mangled Beaumont bled,
And Johnson grinds poor Shakespeare's bones for bread.

Nevertheless, it is clear that Darwin and Johnson could pass as friendly acquaintances before such a shrewd observer as Mrs. Thrale. In the diary of her tour to Wales with Johnson, we find this entry: "The next morning (8 July, 1774) began by breakfasting with Doctor Darwin, a physician of this town, who has an elegant house in it where he entertained us very kindly. . . . At Dr. Darwin's there is a rose-tree as tall as an apple-tree and immensely full of flowers. I counted one hundred, and left so many untold that I was weary of conjecturing the numbers."[1]

If Dr. Johnson's manners jarred on Darwin, there can be little doubt that Dr. Darwin's religious opinions jarred on Johnson. That was probably the beginning and the end of the trouble. The terror of the here-after displayed by the Christian, Johnson, contrasts oddly with the composure of the Pagan, Darwin, at the thought of utter annihilation. Johnson, with his

[1] This rose-tree impressed her so much that, many years later, she wrote from Florence : "I have no roses equal to those at Lichfield, where on one tree I recollect counting eighty-four within my own reach ; it grew against the house of Dr. Darwin."

extraordinary intellectual endowment, must have hated a man who was openly amused by his superstitions; and the contempt of an intellectual equal is, of all things in the world, the hardest to bear. . . .

That Darwin was a wit, and a great wit, is not open to question. Anna Seward's examples of his repartee do not show him at his best, but with such a dearth of Boswelliana we cannot afford to pass them over. She must be allowed to speak for herself:

"Though Dr. Darwin's hesitation in speaking precluded his flow of colloquial eloquence, it did not impede, or at all lessen, the force of that conciser quality, *wit*. Of satiric wit he possessed a very peculiar species. It was neither the death-doing broadside of Dr. Johnson's satire, nor the aurora borealis of Gray. . . ."

She then tells us of a certain clergyman named Robinson—known in Lichfield as "The Rector"—who, "without the slightest hint of infidelity," couldn't help making certain religious matters the subject of his "frolic raillery." But while his clerical brethren treated his slightly impious sallies with indulgence, he was frequently reproved, with cutting sarcasm, by Dr. Darwin, who as a rule showed little veneration for sacred subjects.

"One evening," says Anna, "when he and Dr. Darwin were in company together, the rector had, as usual, thrown the bridle upon the neck of his fancy, and it was scampering over the churchyard and into the chancel, when the doctor exclaimed: 'Excellent! Mr. Robinson is not only a clever fellow, but a *damned* clever fellow!'

"Soon after the subject of common swearing was introduced, Mr. R. made a mock eulogium upon its power to animate dullness, and to season wit. Dr. Darwin observed, 'Christ says, Swear not at *all*. St. Paul tells us we may swear *occasionally*. Mr. Robinson advises us to swear *incessantly*. Let us compromise between these counsellors, and swear by n-non-en-ti-ties. I will swear by my im-pu-dence, and Mr. Robinson by his mo-dest-y.'"

In a letter to William Hayley, dated 23 December, 1784, Anna reports the doctor in more attractive mood. They were walking in a friend's garden and Darwin was descanting on rare and beautiful plants. Suddenly he turned to Anna and asked whether she had seen the plant Kalmia, which had only just been introduced to English greenhouses. She said she had not seen it and asked him to describe it.

"It is a flower of such exquisite beauty," said he, "that would make you waste the summer's day in examining it; you would forget the hour of dinner; all your senses would be absorbed in *one*—you would be all *eye*."

"What," asked Anna with a smile, "is its colour?"

"Precisely that of a seraph's wing," replied Darwin. They laughed, and he added, "I have never set eyes on it, madam."

Darwin's love of botany, by the way, was useful to him as a means of introduction to Rousseau. The latter was living in 1766 at Wooton Hall, and used to spend much of his time in melancholy contemplation in a cave on the terrace. He disliked being interrupted, so Dr. Darwin sauntered by and minutely examined a plant growing in front of it. This drew forth Rousseau, who was keen on botany, and they chatted together for some time, afterwards exchanging letters for several years. . . .

At the age of sixteen, as we have seen, Erasmus had a most unboylike objection to spirits. It was a period, we must remember, when few gentlemen went to bed sober, when General Burgoyne could write to David Garrick begging his "excuse if this is not intelligible, being just risen from rather too much claret." Darwin, as a doctor, was brought into close touch with the physical effects of persistent inebriety, and if he had been asked whether he believed in hell-fire, he would have replied: "Certainly, it rages in the belly of every drunkard."

"From the time at which Dr. Darwin first came to Lichfield," says Miss Seward, "he avowed a conviction of the pernicious effects of all vinous fluid on the youthful and healthy constitution; an absolute horror of spirits of all sorts, and however diluted. His own example, with very few exceptions, supported his exhortations. From strong malt liquor he totally abstained, and if he drank a glass or two of English wine, he mixed it with water. Acid fruits, with sugar, and all sorts of creams and butter were his luxuries; but he always ate plentifully of animal food. This liberal alimentary regimen he prescribed to people of every age, where unvitiated appetite rendered them capable of following it; even to infants. He despised the prejudice which deems foreign wines more wholesome than the wines of the country. If you must drink wine, said he, let it be home-made. It is well known that Dr. Darwin's influence and example have sobered the county of Derby; that intemperance in fermented fluid of every species is almost unknown among its gentlemen."

Yet he was not always inhuman enough to live up to his precepts, as the following anecdote proves:

"Mr. Sneyd . . . and a few more gentlemen of Staffordshire, prevailed upon the doctor to join them in an expedition by water, from Burton to Nottingham, and on to Newark. They had cold provisions on board, and plenty of wine. It was midsummer; the day ardent and sultry. The noontide meal had been made, and the glass gone gayly round. It was one of those *few* instances, in which the medical votary of the Naiads transgressed his general and strict sobriety. If not absolutely intoxicated, his spirits were in a high state of vinous exhilaration. On the boat approaching Nottingham, within the distance of a few fields, he surprised his companions by stepping, without any previous notice, from the boat into the middle of the river, and swimming to shore. They saw him get upon the bank, and walk coolly over the meadows toward the town: they called to him in vain, he did not once turn his head.

"Anxious lest he should take a dangerous cold by remaining in his wet clothes, and uncertain whether or not he intended to desert the party, they rowed instantly to the town, at which they had not designed to have touched, and went in search of their river-god.

"In passing through the market-place they saw him standing upon a tub, encircled by a crowd of people, and resisting the entreaties of an apothecary of the place, one of his old acquaintance, who was importuning him to go to his house, and accept of other raiments till his own could be dried.

"The party, on pressing through the crowd, were surprised to hear him speaking without any degree of his usual stammer:

"'Have I not told you, my friend, that I had drank a considerable quantity of wine before I committed myself to the river? You know my general sobriety; and, as a professional man, you *ought* to know, that the *unusual* existence of *internal* stimulus, would, in its effect upon the system, counteract the *external* cold and moisture.'

"Then, perceiving his companions near him, he nodded, smiled, and waved his hand, as enjoining them silence, thus, without hesitation, addressing the populace:

"'Ye men of Nottingham, listen to me. You are ingenious and industrious mechanics. By your industry life's comforts are procured for yourselves and families. If you lose your health, the power of being industrious will forsake you. *That* you know; but you may *not* know that to breathe fresh and changed air constantly is not less necessary to preserve health than sobriety itself. Air becomes unwholesome in a few hours if the windows are shut. Open those of your sleeping-rooms whenever you quit them to go to your workshops. Keep the windows of your workshops open whenever the weather is not insupportably cold. I have no *interest* in giving you this advice. Remember what I, your countryman, and a physician, tell you. If you would not bring infection and disease upon yourselves, and to your wives and little ones, change the air you breathe, change it many times in a day, by opening your windows.'

"So saying, he stept down from the tub, and returning with his party to their boat, they pursued their voyage."

The men of Nottingham may or may not have opened their windows; but nothing, surely, could have induced them to shut their public-houses after such eloquent testimony to the uplifting quality of " vinous fluid."

In spite of this episode, Darwin was a pioneer of temperance reform, and many years ahead of his time. The oldest temperance societies were founded in North America in 1808, and in Great Britain in 1829.

He must, in fact, have been most intemperate in his advocacy of temperance. According to Maria Edgeworth "he believed that almost all the distempers of the higher classes of people arise from drinking, in some form or other, too much vinous spirit. To this he attributed the aristocratic disease of gout, the jaundice, and all bilious or liver complaints, in short, all the family of pain. This opinion he supported in his writings with all the force of his eloquence and reason; and still more in conversation, by all those powers of wit, satire, and peculiar humour which never appeared fully to the public in his works, but which gained him strong ascendancy in private society. During his lifetime he almost banished wine from the tables of the rich of his acquaintance; and persuaded most of the gentry in his own and the neighbouring counties to become water-drinkers. Partly in jest and partly in earnest, he expressed suspicions, and carried his inferences on this subject, to a preposterous excess. When he heard that my father was bilious, he suspected that this must be the consequence of his having, since his residence in Ireland, and in compliance with the fashion of the country, indulged too freely in drink. His letter, I remember, concluded with: 'Farewell, my dear friend, God keep you from whisky, if he can!' To any one who knew my father, this must seem a laughable suspicion, for he was famous, or in those days, I may say, infamous, in Ireland, for his temperance.''

All the same, the doctor was no bigot. In old age he used to drink two glasses of home-made wine daily because it did him good, and he once advised his friend Josiah Wedgwood "to live as high as your constitution will admit of, in respect to both eating and drinking. This advice could be given to very few people!'' Josiah was not given to self-indulgence. . . .

Though Darwin put as much vigour into the practice of medicine as would have absorbed the sum-total of another man's energy, he yet seemed to have enough time over to interest himself in everything that was going on around him and invent innumerable mechanical contrivances. The expression ''an inquiring and benevolent spirit'' would, with a full modern allowance of superlative, summarize his leading characteristics. To take the inquiring spirit first, let Anna Seward speak:

"In the year 1768, Dr. Darwin met with an accident of irretrievable injury in the human frame. His propensity to mechanics had unfortunately led him to construct a very singular carriage. It was a platform, with a seat fixed upon a very high pair of wheels, and supported in the front, upon the back of the horse, by means of a kind of proboscis, which, forming an arch, reached over the hind-quarters of the horse; and passed through a ring, placed on an upright piece of iron, which worked in a socket, fixed in the saddle. The horse could thus move from one side of the road to the other, quartering, as it is called, at the will of the driver, whose constant attention was necessarily employed to regulate a piece of machinery contrived, but *not well* contrived, for that purpose. From this whimsical carriage the doctor was several times thrown, and the last time he used it, had the misfortune, from a similar accident, to break the patella of his right knee, which caused, as it always must cause, an incurable weakness in the fractured part, and a lameness, not very discernible, indeed, when walking on even ground."

A less dangerous but more remarkable invention of his was a speaking machine. In 1798 Edgeworth wrote to him: "The speaking machine, which is just announced from France, does not say so many words as yours did many years ago." This invention of his, which Edgeworth saw and heard in 1770, "pronounced the *p, b, m,* and the vowel *a,* with so great nicety as to deceive all who heard it unseen, when it pronounced the words *mama, papa, map,* and *pam*; and it had a most plaintive tone, when the lips were gradually closed." It was, at any rate, effective enough for that astute man of business, Matthew Boulton, to enter into an agreement with him over it:

I promise to pay to Dr. Darwin of Lichfield one thousand pounds upon his delivering to me (within two years of date hereof) an Instrument call'd an organ that is capable of pronouncing the Lord's prayer, the creed, and ten Commandments in the vulgar tongue and his ceding to me and me only the property of the sd invention with all the advantages thereunto appertaining.

M. BOULTON, Soho, Sep. 3rd 1777.

Witness : JAMES KEIR.
Witness : W. SMALL.

In the eighteenth century a speaking-tube was unknown in country districts, but Dr. Darwin had one from his study to the kitchen. A countryman had brought a letter to his house and was sitting alone in the kitchen waiting for an answer, when suddenly a sepulchral voice said almost in his ear, "I want some coals." He fled for his life, and nothing on earth could ever induce him to go near the house again, for the doctor had the reputation among the country folk of being a bit of a wizard. . . .

At a time when artesian wells were practically unknown in this country, Erasmus made one in his garden. He also designed a horizontal windmill for grinding flints, which Wedgwood used with success. His Commonplace Book is full of ideas and sketches for lamps, candlesticks with telescope-stands, knitting-looms, weighing and surveying machines, water-closets, and what-not. He noted down that "a machine to measure the quantity of air passing from North to South or from South to North is not impossible to construct"—and he promptly drew a diagram. His fancy played round the subject of visible or luminous music; fogs and frosts engaged his keen attention; his mind jumped from electricity to wooden chessmen, from a double-furrow plough to an artificial bird, from perpetual motion to diving-bells, from vegetation to evaporation.

He invented a manifold writer, which gave Watt the idea of his copying-machine. He planned a canal lock, the principle of which was acted on many years later. He designed a rotary pump, which was afterwards extensively used. He was the first to perceive that the spokes of carriage wheels could be made to act as springs. And it was he who made a shrewd guess concerning the composition of water which first put Watt on the track of his great discovery.

He never tired of speculating on the weather and the direction of the winds, noting each change and variation as it occurred; for which purpose he connected a wind-vane on the top of his house with a dial on the ceiling of his study. He thought it possible that the winds might be governed by human agency, and he suggested a method whereby man could improve the climatic conditions of his planet:

"If the nations who inhabit this hemisphere of the globe, instead of destroying their seamen and exhausting their wealth in unnecessary wars, could be induced to unite their labours to navigate the immense masses of ice in the polar regions into the more southern oceans, two great advantages would result to mankind; the tropic countries would be much cooled by their solution, and our winters in this latitude would be rendered much milder for perhaps a century or two, till the masses of ice became again enormous."

His experiments covered every field of human endeavour; all knowledge was his province. Even as a physician he recognized no boundary to his investigations. The following paragraph, which appeared in a local paper on 23 October, 1762, gives us a curious glimpse into the eighteenth century:

"The body of the malefactor, who is ordered to be executed in Lichfield on Monday the 25th inst. will afterwards be conveyed to the house of Dr. Darwin, who will begin a course of anatomical lectures at four o'clock on Tuesday evening, and continue them every day as long as the body can be preserved; and shall be glad to be favoured with the company of any who profess medicine or surgery, or whom the love of science may induce."

Let us now turn to another and equally prominent aspect of Dr. Darwin's character—his benevolence. All his friends testify to this with an unexampled chorus of praise. "Great author as you are, my dear Doctor," writes Edgeworth to him, "I think you excel the generality of mankind as much in generosity as in abilities." And at a later date Edgeworth declared: "I have known him intimately during thirty-six years, and in that period have witnessed innumerable instances of his benevolence." Another lifelong friend, James Keir, emphasizes this: "I think all those who knew him will allow that sympathy and benevolence were the most striking features. He felt very sensibly for others, and, from his knowledge of human nature, he entered into their feelings and sufferings in the different circumstances of their constitution, character, health, sickness, and prejudice. In benevolence, he thought that almost all virtues consisted. He despised the monkish abstinences and the hypocritical pretensions which so often impose on the world. The communication of happiness and the relief of misery were by him held as the only standard of moral merit. Though he extended his humanity to every sentient being, it was not like that of some philosophers, so diffused as to be of no effect; but his affection was there warmest where it could be of most service to his family and his friends, who will long remember the constancy of his attachment and his zeal for their welfare."

Finally Anna Seward must have her word: "Professional generosity distinguished Dr. Darwin's medical practice. While resident in Lichfield, to the priest and lay-vicars of its cathedral, and their families, he always cheerfully gave his advice, but never took fees from any of them. Diligently, also, did he attend to the health of the poor in that city, and afterwards at Derby, and supplied their necessities by food, and all sort of charitable assistance. In each of those towns, *his* was the cheerful board of almost open-housed hospitality, without extravagance or parade; deeming ever the first unjust, the latter unmanly. Generosity, wit, and science, were his household gods."

Perhaps his essential sympathy and kindness of heart

were never more strikingly illustrated than in a letter he wrote in 1767 to a gentleman who had consulted him about the body of an illegitimate child, which had been murdered by its mother:

Dear Sir,

I am sorry you should think it necessary to make any excuse for the Letter I this morning received from you,—The Cause of Humanity needs no Apology to me. . . .

The Women that have committed this most unnatural Crime, are real Objects of our greatest Pity;—their Education has produced in them so much Modesty, or Sense of Shame, y^t this artificial Passion overturns the very Instincts of Nature ! What struggles must there be in their Minds, what agonies ! and at a Time when, after the pains of Parturition, Nature has designed them the sweet consolation of giving Suck to a little helpless Babe, that depends on them for its hourly existence !

The cause of this most horrid crime is an Excess of what is really a Virtue, of the Sense of Shame or Modesty. Such is the condition of human Nature !

I have carefully avoided the use of scientific terms in this letter, y^t you might make any use of it you may think proper, and shall only add y^t I am veryly convinced of the Truth of every part of it,

> and am, dear Sr.,
> your affect. Friend and Servt.
> ERASMUS DARWIN.

Two well-authenticated stories will attest the gratitude of the poor to him.

On his way to visit a patient, he stopped for the night at Newmarket, where the races were in full swing and the town was in an uproar. He managed to get a room in the hotel, and went to bed early, tired out.

In the middle of the night he woke up suddenly and saw his bedroom door quietly opening. He jumped up and challenged the intruder. Instantly a man slipped into his room, closed the door quickly behind him, and begged the doctor not to make a sound, as he had only come to do him a good turn. He then tiptoed to the bed and spoke in a whisper:

" I have not come to rob you but to pay you back for your kindness to my wife. You attended her in a long illness without a fee; I have always meant to show you my gratitude, but never had a chance till now."

He informed the doctor that he was riding the favourite in the big race on the following day, that everyone was betting on it, but that he had had instructions not to let it win. He then gave the doctor the name of the horse that was going to win, advised him to put his last shilling on it, and withdrew as quietly as he had come.

The doctor went to sleep again and by the next morning had forgotten all about the big race. He only recalled the incident when he was told, on his way back through Newmarket, that the favourite had lost and that the horse the man had begged him to back had romped home first. . . .

Some years after, the doctor was riding late at night along the road to Nottingham. At one point, where the road passed through a wood, the darkness was intense. There was a clatter behind him, and a mounted man came abreast of him. The doctor greeted him with "A fine night." The man, after peering in silence at him for a moment, spurred his horse and passed on without speaking. Some minutes elapsed; the road left the trees; and there, just ahead of him, was the same man riding very slowly.

The doctor came up with him, again hailed him, was again subjected to the man's scrutiny, but received no answer and passed on.

A few days after this incident a traveller was held up and robbed near the same wood, and the robber was captured. Struck by the description of the robber and the coincidence of the locality, Dr. Darwin visited the fellow in prison, who, when tackled on the subject, admitted he was the same man. Naturally the doctor wanted to know why he hadn't attempted to rob him. After a short silence, the man replied:

"I thought it was you when I heard your voice the first time; I knew it was you when you spoke the second time; and I could not rob a man who had saved my mother's life, and kept her in food while she was ill, and never charged her a penny."

It is not surprising, then, that Darwin should have inspired some lines by his friend, Sir Brooke Boothby, which are perhaps more valuable as a statement than as a sonnet:

> If bright example more than precept sway,
> Go, take your lesson from the life of Day,
> Or, Darwin, thine whose ever-open door
> Draws, like Bethesda's pool, the suffering poor,
> Where some fit cure the wretched all obtain,
> Relieved at once from poverty and pain.

CHAPTER IV

ENTER EDGEWORTH

In the autumn of the year 1765 the ladies and gentlemen of Chester and the country round about were in
a state of great excitement over the Microcosm, a
mechanical exhibition of moving pictures. The move-
ments of the figures, both men and animals, were
considered highly ingenious, and the various motions
of the heavenly bodies were represented with so much
neatness and precision that the gay life of the city was
almost suspended, while the exhibition was crowded
day after day by the nobility and gentry, who could
talk of nothing else for weeks.

Among the visitors was a young spark from Ireland
named Richard Lovell Edgeworth. He was staying in
Chester for a few days with his wife and was so en-
thralled by the Microcosm that nothing could keep him
away from it. At last he prevailed upon the manager
to show him the internal structure of the whole
machinery, and in the course of conversation he
elicited the fact that a certain Dr. Darwin of Lichfield
had been interested in the Microcosm and was himself
the inventor of many ingenious things: for example, a
carriage which was '' so constructed as to turn in a
small compass, without danger of oversetting, and
without the encumbrance of a crane-necked perch.''

Now it so happened that young Edgeworth was just then at a loose end. He had been flirting with the idea of entering Parliament; but upon hearing of Dr. Darwin's carriage, he dismissed every political ambition from his mind and determined to try his skill at coach-making, with the object of obtaining similar advantages in a carriage of his own construction. He therefore took a house on Hare Hatch Common, between Reading and Maidenhead, and commenced a life of experiments.

Richard Lovell Edgeworth was born in 1744. He came of a family that had been resident in Ireland since the reign of Elizabeth. At the age of five, in a fit of temper, he threw a box-iron, complete with red-hot heater, at the head of his elder brother, who ducked and avoided it in the nick of time. The shock, together with a serious sermon from his mother, did Richard a lot of good, and in after life the equable-ness of his temper was the most distinctive part of his character.

In due time he went to Trinity College, Dublin, where for once in his life he behaved as other men did. That is to say, he passed his time " in dissipation of every kind." At the end of six months he abandoned " copious potations" in disgust, and was able to say in later years that he had never been intoxicated in his life, though he had taken part in four or five contested elections.

From Dublin he went to Oxford, where he resided with a gentleman named Elers, and carried matters to such lengths with one of the gentleman's daughters that he was forced to marry her, becoming a father before he was twenty. Excepting only a passion for the other sex, which brought upon him four marriages and twenty-two children, Edgeworth seems from his own account to have been a model young man and a model middle-aged man, and from his daughter Maria's account a model old man into the bargain. His keen interest in mechanics, his inventive faculties, his polished manners, his natural gaiety, and a certain facility in friendship, gained him the esteem and affection of many worthy men. His *Memoirs* are commendably candid, admirably written, and contain a more varied picture of his period than any book except Boswell's.

While living on Hare Hatch Common he kept several terms at the Temple, read scientific books, constructed a carriage, played cards, made experiments, and lived on an allowance from his father. He was introduced to the gay and gambling world by Sir Francis Delaval, a notorious rake of the period, and together they concocted a scheme whereby the results of the Newmarket races could be received in London by a system of telegraphic communication long before they could arrive in the ordinary way. Some of his inventions were more curious than useful. One was a sailing carriage, which threatened to distribute the horse traffic on the roads about Reading in a most alarming manner. Another was a giant wooden horse, which, by a strange arrangement of front and rear legs, could carry him safely over any wall in the country. He experimented on this at intervals for forty years, but never achieved complete success. A third was a huge hollow wheel, by walking within which a man could travel much faster than his legs could naturally take him. This interesting novelty was wrecked before completion by a small boy, who got into it and began to ply his legs. The wheel, helped by a gentle incline, needed no human encouragement and dashed off in the direction of a chalk-pit. The boy saved his life by jumping out, but the wheel refused to be saved and was picked up in small fragments the following morning by its sorrowful contriver, who had not enough capital to give the experiment a further trial.

Edgeworth's main interest at this time was, however, the carriage which he was making on the hint given him at Chester concerning Dr. Darwin's invention. He spent whole days in his workshop; he visited the smiths and coachmakers at Reading continuously; and at last the job was completed. He drove to London in a "very handsome phaeton," constructed on the Darwinian principle, and showed it to the Society for the Encouragement of Arts, etc. The society approved the invention—and the rest must be told in Edgeworth's words:

"I wrote an account to the doctor of the reception which his scheme had met with from the Society of Arts, etc. The doctor wrote me a very civil answer; and though, as I afterwards found out, he took me for a coachmaker, he invited me to his house. An invitation which I accepted in the ensuing summer.

"When I arrived at Lichfield, I went to inquire whether the doctor was at home. I was shown into a room, where I found Mrs. Darwin. I told her my name. She said the doctor expected me, and that he intended to be at home before night. There were books and prints in the room, of which I took occasion to speak. Mrs. Darwin asked me to drink tea, and I perceived that I owed to my literature the pleasure of passing the evening with this most agreeable woman. We walked and conversed upon various literary subjects till it was dark, when Mrs. Darwin seemed to be surprised that the doctor had not come home. I offered to take my leave; but she told me, that I had been expected for some days, and that a bed had been prepared for me; I heard some orders given to the housemaid, who had destined a different room for my reception from that which her mistress had upon second thoughts appointed. I perceived that the maid examined me attentively, but I could not guess the reason. When supper was nearly finished, a loud rapping at the door announced the doctor. There was a bustle in the hall, which made Mrs. Darwin get up and go to the door. Upon her exclaiming, that they were bringing in a dead man, I went to the hall; I saw some persons, directed by one whom I guessed to be Doctor Darwin, carrying a man who appeared motionless.

" ' He is not dead,' said Doctor Darwin; ' he is only dead drunk. I found him,' continued the doctor, ' nearly suffocated in a ditch; I had him lifted into my carriage, and brought hither, that we might take care of him to-night.'

" Candles came, and what was the surprise of the doctor, and of Mrs. Darwin, to find that the person whom he had saved was Mrs. Darwin's brother! who, for the first time in his life, as I was assured, had been intoxicated in this manner, and who would undoubtedly have perished, had it not been for Doctor Darwin's humanity.

" During this scene I had time to survey my new friend, Doctor Darwin. He was a large man, fat, and rather clumsy; but intelligence and benevolence were painted in his countenance; he had a considerable impediment in his speech, a defect which is in general painful to others; but the doctor repaid his auditors so well for making them wait for his wit or his knowledge, that he seldom found them impatient.

" When his brother was disposed of, he came to supper, and I thought that he looked at Mrs. Darwin, as if he was somewhat surprised, when he heard that I had passed the whole evening in her company. After she withdrew, he entered into conversation with me upon the carriage that I had made, and upon the remarks that fell from some members of the society to whom I had shown it. I satisfied his curiosity, and having told him, that my carriage was in the town, and that he could see it whenever he pleased, we talked upon other mechanical subjects, and afterwards on various branches of knowledge, which necessarily produced allusions to classical literature; by these he discovered that I had received the education of a gentleman.

" ' Why! I thought,' said the doctor, ' that you were only a coach-maker!'—' That was the reason,' said I, ' that you looked surprised at finding me at supper with Mrs. Darwin. But you see, Doctor, how superior in discernment ladies are even to the most

learned gentlemen; I assure you, that I had not been
in the room five minutes, before Mrs. Darwin asked
me to tea.'

" The next day I was introduced to some literary
persons, who then resided at Lichfield, and among the
foremost to Miss Seward. How much of my future
life has depended upon this visit to Lichfield! How
little could I then foresee, that my having examined
and understood the Microcosm at Chester should lead
me to a place, and into an acquaintance, which would
otherwise, in all human probability, have never fallen
within my reach! Miss Seward was at this time in the
height of youth and beauty, of an enthusiastic temper,
a votary of the muses, and of the most eloquent and
brilliant conversation. Our mutual acquaintance was
soon made, and it continued to be for many years of
my life a source of never-failing pleasure. It seems
that Mrs. Darwin had a little pique against Miss
Seward, who had in fact been her rival with the doctor.
These ladies lived upon good terms, but there frequently occurred little competitions, which amused
their friends, and enlivened the uniformity that so often
renders a country town insipid. The evening after my
arrival, Mrs. Darwin invited Miss Seward, and a very
large party of her friends, to supper. I was placed
beside Miss Seward, and a number of lively sallies
escaped her, that set the table in good humour. I
remember, for we frequently remember the merest
trifles which happen at an interesting period of our
lives, that she repeated some of Prior's *Henry and
Emma*, of which she was always fond, and dwelling

upon Emma's tenderness, she cited the care that Emma proposed to take of her lover, if he were wounded:

To bind his wounds my finest lawns I'll tear,
Wash them with tears, and wipe them with my hair.

" I acknowledged, that tearing her finest lawns, even in a wild forest, would be a real sacrifice from a fine lady; and that washing wounds with salt water, though a very severe remedy, was thought to be salutary; but I could not think, that wiping them with her hair could be either a salutary or an elegant operation. I represented, that the lady, who must have had by her own account a choice of lawns, might have employed some of the coarse sort for this operation, instead of having recourse to her hair. I paid Miss Seward, however, some compliments on her own beautiful tresses, and at that moment the watchful Mrs. Darwin took this opportunity of drinking *Mrs. Edgeworth's health*. Miss Seward's surprise was manifest. But the mirth this unexpected discovery made fell but lightly upon its objects, for Miss Seward, with perfect good humour, turned the laugh in her favour. The next evening the same society assembled at another house, and for several ensuing evenings I passed my time in different agreeable companies in Lichfield."

Eighteenth-century provincial society evidently had its moments of devastating playfulness, not without solace to the soul of a philosopher. But what did Lichfield society think of its chronicler? Miss Seward kindly obliges us:

" About the year 1765, came to Lichfield, from the

neighbourhood of Reading, the young and gay philosopher, Mr. Edgeworth, a man of fortune, and recently married to a Miss Elers of Oxfordshire. The fame of Dr. Darwin's various talents allured Mr. E. to the city they graced. Then scarcely two-and-twenty, and with an exterior yet more juvenile, he had mathematic science, mechanic ingenuity, and a competent portion of classical learning, with the possession of the modern languages. His address was gracefully spirited, and his conversation eloquent. He danced, he fenced, and winged his arrows with more than philosophic skill; yet did not the consciousness of these lighter endowments abate his ardour in the pursuit of knowledge."

Dr. Darwin took to Edgeworth at once and wasted no time in getting some of his ingenious friends to meet him. There is proof of his quick interest:

Dear Boulton,

I have got with me a mechanical friend, Mr. Edgeworth, from Oxfordshire—the greatest conjurer I ever saw. God send fine weather, and pray come to my assistance, and prevail on Dr. Small and Mrs. Boulton to attend you to-morrow morning, and we will reconvey you to Birmingham if the devil permit. Edgeworth has the principles of nature in his palm, and moulds them as he pleases—can take away polarity, or give it to the needle by rubbing it thrice on the palm of his hand ! And can see through two solid oak boards without glasses ! Wonderful ! Astonishing ! ! Diabolical ! ! ! Pray tell Dr. Small he must come to see these miracles. Adieu.

E. DARWIN.

In this way Edgeworth became familiar with Matthew Boulton, "the father of Birmingham," as he was called, who was just on the point of moving " to the wild heath, which has since been converted into a garden, interspersed with cheerful villas, by his talents and energy.'' Present - day visitors to Birmingham will have difficulty in recognizing from Edgeworth's description the locality known as Soho.

Dr. Darwin had become intimate with Boulton shortly after his arrival at Lichfield, and they remained close friends all their lives. Boulton is chiefly remembered by a modern generation as the partner of James Watt. But if it had not been for Boulton, it is highly probable that Watt's steam-engine would never have seen the light of day. Boulton founded the Soho works with the dower he obtained with his wife; and he needed a steam-engine for his works just as much as Watt needed a works for his steam-engine. The invention of the engine was due to Watt, the introduction to Boulton. In fact Boulton brought himself to the verge of bankruptcy before the engine was a commercial success. In addition to his business foresight, he possessed something that was even more valuable for a man with the temperament of his partner —a confiding, generous, and optimistic spirit. Watt, with his chronic bad health, was constantly down in the dumps. Boulton cheered him and encouraged him and forced him to believe in himself, begging him again and again to pray morning and evening '' The Lord grant us a gude conceit of ourselves.'' There is a letter that Boulton wrote to Watt in 1781 which paints the writer to the life:

I am sure it is impossible we can disagree in the settling of our accounts, as there is no sum total in any of them that I value so much as I do your esteem, and the promotion of your health and happiness ; therefore I will not raise a single objection to anything that you shall think just, as I have a most implicit confidence in your honour.

Shortly after their introduction, Edgeworth went to stay with Boulton at his house on Snow Hill, Birmingham, and was shown over the principal manufactories. "There, and at Soho, I became in a few hours intimately acquainted with many parts of practical mechanics, which I could not otherwise have learned in many months."

He returned to Hare Hatch with mechanics on the brain. He invented a new carriage, a wagon, a large umbrella for covering haystacks, a turnip-cutter, a perambulator. For these he received the gold and silver medals of the Society for the Encouragement of Arts, etc. He carried his experiments into the domestic circle, and educated his son according to the system of Rousseau: that is to say, the body and mind of the lad were left to educate themselves, so that he gradually acquired "all the virtues of a child bred in the hut of a savage," and developed an unfortunate tendency to disobey instructions.

The fever for experiment that possessed Edgeworth led him into extravagance. The making of carriages, and possibly even of turnip-cutters, required capital; so he wrote to Dr. Darwin for a loan of £1000. The doctor, knowing nothing whatever of Edgeworth's affairs, sent it by return.

CHAPTER V

DAY

As time went on Edgeworth's experiments were diversified by the arrival in his neighbourhood of a young gentleman named Day, who was home from Oxford on his holidays. Day became famous in after-years as the author of *Sandford and Merton*, upon which three generations of British school-children were nurtured. It is impossible for the biographer of any member of the Darwinian circle to refrain from casting at least one longing, lingering look at Thomas Day, and wondering whether Thomas is not a more promising subject than the one he has undertaken. The present biographer will not pretend for a moment that he has not been severely tempted by Day from his path of duty to Darwin. Indeed, he has, in a sense succumbed; for this chapter is about Day, not Darwin. But he has good excuses for the lapse.

Firstly, Day and Darwin were the only noteworthy writers and poets of an almost exclusively scientific circle. Secondly, though enjoying an enormous popularity in their own age, they are almost entirely neglected in ours. Thirdly, they were constantly bracketed together by their friends as the two most remarkable personalities and the two most benevolent men of their time. We have already seen them placed side by side

48

in a sonnet by Boothby. And James Keir, who wrote Day's *Life*, said that Darwin retained "more of his original character than almost any man I have known, excepting, perhaps, Mr. Day. Indeed, the originality of character in both these men was too strong to give way to the example of others."

Fourthly, it is a curious fact that both men inspired their friends to write biographies of them. Edgeworth wished to write on Day, but was forestalled by Keir; he then wished to write on Darwin, but was forestalled by Miss Seward. (The number of people who were going to write on Darwin, but never did, suggests an interesting biographical problem, which has puzzled and dismayed at least one earnest student.)

Fifthly, the contrast between the two men is so striking that one wonders how they could possibly have had the same circle of friends, and above all how they could have remained on friendly terms with one another.

Both were sound humanitarians. Both hated injustice and were strong in their advocacy of the rights of man. Both had an utter contempt for Parliament and politicians. Neither subscribed to the orthodox religion, though both were intensely religious. Their humanity and benevolence expressed itself in deeds no less than in words; they were practical and unostentatious philanthropists. Yet their human relationships were of a vastly different nature, and their ordinary social feelings and actions were radically dissimilar. Darwin was a realist; Day was an idealist.

Their comments on one another reveal them both.

Day said of Darwin: " He is one of the three friends from whom I have met with constant kindness." Darwin said of Day: " He was dear to me by many names, as friend, philosopher, scholar and honest man." A brief sketch of Day's life may therefore illustrate, more vividly than anything else, the humour, sympathy, and humanity of Dr. Darwin. . . .

Thomas Day was born on 22 June, 1748, in Well-close Square, London. His father died less than a year after his birth and left him an estate of £1200 a year at Bear Hill, near Wargrave, in Berkshire, with a jointure of £300 a year to his mother. Six years later his mother married again—one Thomas Phillips, of the Custom House, who contrived to get on his stepson's nerves to such an extent that the latter preferred school to home. At a much later period Day described his stepfather as " one of those common characters who seek to supply their inherent want of consequence by a busy teasing interference in circumstances with which they have no real concern." Nevertheless, when he came of age, Day increased his mother's jointure to £400 and settled it on her and her husband for their lives. This was characteristic of him, for he was a philanthropist out of contempt as much as out of kindness.

He was, however, fond of his mother, whose Spartan character has been embalmed in an anecdote by Keir. Once, in her maiden days, she was walking through a field with a friend, when they were approached by a bull " with all the marks of malevolence." The friend began to run, but Thomas's mother was made of sterner stuff. She stood her ground, eyed the bull squarely and severely, and the bull, possibly with some precognition of Thomas, spared her.

Thomas showed early signs of a disquieting inquisitiveness. His mother exhorted him to read the Bible, and he did so. The Book of Revelation appealed to him at the age of seven or thereabouts, and his imagination was fired by the whore of Babylon. But his mother refused to satisfy his desire for information relative to the lady and referred him to the rector, who scarcely felt equal to the occasion and told him that the phrase was "allegorical." Thomas thought this a feeble way out of the difficulty and promptly informed his mother that the rector didn't know what he was talking about. It is not recorded that stepfather Phillips interfered at this juncture.

Charterhouse received Thomas in due course, but he was never a characteristic Carthusian. For example, he gave away his pocket money to the poor and was noted for his kindness to animals. He was British enough to learn boxing, but not boyish enough to beat his opponent; for once, when he was fighting a fellow who had no chance against him, he called the fight off, and shook hands. His holidays were mostly spent at Bear Hill, where, according to Blackman, " he would gather a posy of wild flowers and enjoy the song of the lark as she carolled on her ethereal way, but his sensitive spirit would not permit him to rob a poor bird's nest."

His fondness for animals was conspicuous throughout his life, and his consideration for them was the cause of his death. Keir says that Day would willingly have been a vegetarian if he had not decided that "the practice of rearing and killing animals for food was productive of more happiness than of pain to them; as the existence of most of them is owing to this practice, and their lives, though shortened, are rendered comfortable by the indulgence of their appetites, while no fears of the deaths to which they are destined disturb their repose." This seems about as good an excuse for eating *pâté de foie gras* as any one has come across.

Day went to Oxford, where for three years he studied philosophy and drank water, but left without a degree. It was during one of his college vacations that he met Richard Lovell Edgeworth, who was living at Hare Hatch near by. They took to one another immediately, in spite of the fact that their tastes were dissimilar. Day was a serious and melancholy person, who hated frivolity and distrusted women. Edgeworth was a gay dog, especially among the women. Mrs. Edgeworth (the first) did not like Day. To begin with, he never brushed his hair, his manners were uncouth, and he dressed anyhow. Worse still, he denounced the charms of female society. Worst of all, he spent hours every day discussing metaphysics with her husband. Edgeworth could never understand his wife's attitude. "She lamented about trifles," says he, "and the lamenting of a female with whom we live does not render home delightful." The question is: Was the enforced company of Mr. Day a trifle? We shall see.

Though Day was suspicious of the female sex, and recoiled from the Capuan horrors of a minuet, he never so far abandoned hope in humanity as to believe there were no women worthy of him. Indeed, a large portion of his life was spent in the search for a lady "wiser than the rest of her sex, who should feel for him the most romantic and everlasting attachment—a paragon, who should forget the follies and vanities of her sex for him." Such a one he thought he had found during a walking-tour in the west of England about this time. But upon being informed, in polished eighteenth-century verse, that she would be expected to live with him "sequestered in some secret grove," the lady demurred and finally declined the honour.

Shaken but by no means shattered, Thomas pursued his investigations elsewhere. In the spring of 1768 he visited Ireland with Edgeworth. The manner of their going was peculiar and proves that young gentlemen of the eighteenth century were as light-hearted and light-headed as those of any other century. They travelled in a phaeton. Edgeworth's son, aged five, was with them. To amuse themselves on the journey they agreed that Day should pass for a very odd gentle-man (apparently it never struck them that he would not have to act the part) who was travelling about the world to overcome his sorrow for the loss of his wife, that Edgeworth's boy should pass as the extraordinary child of the odd gentleman, and that Edgeworth himself should play the part of servant and factotum.

The drama commenced at Eccleshall, in Stafford-shire, where Edgeworth drove up the street with great éclat, pulled up at the inn, and bawled for the hostler. Having disposed of his "master," Edgeworth went into the kitchen to order dinner. He inspected the larder, much to the landlady's amazement, and made a clean sweep of every delicacy it contained. He then went outside with his son and diverted the populace with several exhibitions of physical activity, winding up the entertainment with a long account of his "master's" oddity. After this he returned to the kitchen and superintended the preparation of his dinner. It is difficult to say how long the pleasantries of the party would have been indulged, for at this point Dr. Erasmus Darwin made an unexpected appearance, greeted Edgeworth by name, and thus put a period to the eccentricities of the trio. Day was introduced to Darwin, but their acquaintance did not begin favourably. The conversation between Darwin and Edgeworth was about mechanical matters; it lasted for several hours; and as Day had no taste for such things, he "did not join in"—which is probably Edgeworth's polite way of saying that he sulked. However, the experts were considerate enough to start some other topic before the meeting dispersed, and "Mr. Day displayed so much knowledge, feeling, and eloquence" that the doctor invited him to Lichfield. This led to Day's inclusion in the Darwin circle.

Day was disgusted with Dublin and made so many unpleasant remarks about the condition of the poor in the country districts that Edgeworth became a little peevish. What with one thing and another, poor Edgeworth seems to have had a pretty dismal holiday, for when they arrived at his father's house, Day failed to make himself welcome. Edgeworth senior objected to his table-manners, decided he was not a gentleman, and treated him with scant consideration. It is a pity Edgeworth does not specify Day's habits at table. Nothing is so damaging in biography as a general statement, which often implies a multitude of misdemeanours. If Day balanced peas on his knife, Edgeworth should have said so. If he wolfed his food, the fact should have been noted. As it is, one suspects the worst. The phrase, "My father conceived a violent prejudice against him in consequence of something in his manner of eating and sitting at table," suggests unspeakable horrors. One instantly pictures Day sprawling over the table between courses, reaching for the salt under the nose of someone who is in the act of feeding and who nearly chokes to death in consequence, wiping his mouth on the table-cloth, dropping the vegetables down somebody's neck, masticating clamorously, spitting into the soup, picking his teeth with a fork, flicking crumbs into the butler's face, and making stable-sounds when otherwise disengaged. We are told that Day "smiled with philosophic indifference" at his host's "prejudice in favour of politeness," which really makes matters worse, for it hints that Edgeworth senior's mild protest against his guest's habit of paring his nails with the carving-knife was met by Day with a polite "Dear, dear! How silly of me! I keep forgetting that we are in Ireland."

"My sister," said Edgeworth, "stood aloof, while my friend preserved an awful distance from a woman whom he was inclined to consider as a confirmed fine lady, a sort of being for which he had a feeling of something like horror." But as time went on this feeling wore off. Within three months Day was making reference to the "secret grove" which had had such an unsettling effect on his first love. It seems that Miss Edgeworth could have faced sequestration with equanimity, but objected to his personal appearance. If only he would comb his hair and smarten up his gait and garments, she might favourably consider the matter. Edgeworth senior groaned at the prospect but was forced to admit that Mr. Day's morals and fortune were a sound set-off to his objectionable manners and philosophy. It was finally arranged that a year should elapse before the subject was reopened. To please Thomas, Miss Edgeworth agreed to spend the year studying metaphysics, and to please Miss Edgeworth, Thomas promised to study the graces. The two friends returned to London in the autumn. But while the graces did not sit lightly on Thomas, metaphysics sat too heavily on Miss Edgeworth; and before the year was out the arrangement was mutually terminated.

Having left Oxford, Day now had to choose a career. For some years he had been soaking himself in Rousseau, with the result that he wished to work for the melioration of mankind—so he began to study the science of medicine. But in a little while he came to the conclusion that the risk of prescribing wrong medicines far outweighed the good he might do by administering the right ones, and he turned his attention to law. In his opinion bad laws produced bad people, and he was anxious to scrap the feudal absurdities in which the good laws had become entangled. He therefore entered the Temple and began a course of study with this desirable end in view. His sense of the sanctity of life—human and otherwise—did not desert him even in the Temple. "Day, kill that spider!" said a fellow-student on one occasion. "No," replied Day, " I don't know that I have a right. Suppose that a superior being said to a companion, ' Kill that lawyer,' how should you like it? And a lawyer is more noxious to most people than a spider."

In spite of his legal surroundings Day never lost sight of the fact that he was, first and foremost, a human being; and as (we hear from Keir) he retained throughout life " a strong detestation of female seduction," it became more and more necessary that he should marry. The problem was not without difficulties. "He proposed," says Keir, " to unite the purity of female virtue with the fortitude and hardness of constitution of a Spartan virgin, and with a simplicity of taste that should despise the frivolous vanities, the effeminate manners and the dissipated pleasures " which, in the opinion of Rousseau, disgraced the female character of that age. Further, "he resolved"—Anna Seward informs us—"that his wife should have a taste for literature and science, for moral and patriotic philosophy. So might she be his companion in that retirement to which he had destined himself, and assist him in forming the minds of his children to stubborn virtue and high exertion"—for he " loved to mould the infant and youthful mind."

Among other things, he wanted his wife to be as

"simple as a mountain girl, in her dress, her diet, and her manners; fearless and intrepid as the Spartan wives and Roman heroines."

He came to the conclusion that the eighteenth century was strangely lacking in such damsels as he pictured. Anna Seward herself admits that "there was no finding such a creature ready made," so we are not driven to take Day's partial word for it. Regretfully, therefore, he decided to "mould some infant into the being his fancy had imaged."

With a barrister friend, Mr. Bicknel, he descended upon the town of Shrewsbury, and, armed with credentials of his moral probity, visited the Foundling Hospital there. From among "the prattling inmates of that institution" (to quote Blackman) he selected a girl aged eleven—Anna Seward describes her as "a clear, auburn brunette, with dark eyes, glowing bloom and chestnut tresses"—whom he called Sabrina Sidney. (She owed her Christian name to the River Severn and her surname to Day's hero, Algernon.) Day and Bicknel then visited the Foundling Hospital in London, where they selected another girl, aged twelve—described by Anna as "fair, with flaxen locks and light eyes"— and called her Lucretia. Both girls were obtained on written conditions, for which Mr. Bicknel was surety, viz. that within a year Day should apprentice one of them to some trade and support her till she married or set up in business for herself, when he should give her £400. The other he fully intended to retain and educate with a view to marrying her; but if, later on, he decided not to marry her, he promised to maintain her in some "creditable family" until she married, when he undertook to give her £500. During the process of education, he "solemnly engaged never to violate her innocence."

Human nature being what it was (and possibly is), Day's philanthropic scheme was entirely misunderstood by his less virtuous friends and neighbours. Very soon it became advisable for him to remove his wards from "some court near Chancery Lane" and ship them to France, where eccentricity, especially in an Englishman, stood a better chance of passing unnoticed. He settled down at Avignon, where his curious mode of life "excited much surprise," though his excessive generosity gained golden opinions from all and sundry.

He kept his two pupils in total ignorance of the French language, so that they should not be "exposed to any impertinent interference; and as that knowledge of the world from which he wished to preserve them was at one entrance quite shut out, he had their minds entirely open to such ideas and sentiments, and such only, as he desired to implant." Edgeworth tells us that the only qualities he desired in a wife were "simplicity, perfect innocence and attachment to himself." Sabrina and Lucretia were churlish enough not to appreciate the modesty of his requirements. They teased and perplexed him continually; they quarrelled and fought with one another incessantly; they even caught smallpox and made him sit by their bedside night after night. Sometimes he would try to leave their room on tip-toe to get a breath of fresh air outside, but as sure as fate one or other of them would wake up and begin to scream the house down. They would allow no one but Day near them, and he was forced "to perform for them the lowest offices of assistance."

The disease left them unmarked, but his troubles were not yet over. Crossing the Rhone with them one day the boat turned turtle and he had to save them both "with difficulty and danger to himself." Then, at Lyons, a young French officer spoke to the girls with a freedom that this disciple of Rousseau could not brook. He challenged the officer to mortal combat, saying that he would defend their minds no less than their persons from insult, at the risk of his life. The youngster was astounded and instantly disavowed the least intention to offend. He was let off with a caution.

Day did not like the French people. In a letter to Edgeworth he refers to them in these terms: "If true happiness consists in perfect vacuity, they certainly have the advantage of us." And in another letter he sums up the situation thus: "But the most disgusting sight of all is to see that sex, whose weakness of body and imbecility of mind can only entitle them to our compassion and indulgence, assuming an unnatural dominion, and regulating the customs, the manners, the lives and opinions of the other sex, by their own caprices, weakness and ignorance." One has a shrewd suspicion that he means women.

After eight months' wear and tear, Day returned to England. He had decided that his pupils, when together, were too much of a handful; and as Lucretia was both stupid and rebellious, he apprenticed her to a milliner; and when, at a later date, she married a linen-draper, he gave her, as per contract, £400. Sabrina, after a few months in the care of Mr. Bicknel's mother, accompanied Day to Lichfield, where, in order to be near Dr. Darwin, he had taken " the pleasant mansion in Stowe Valley" for twelve months.

This was the spring of 1770. Anna Seward gives a description of Day as he first appeared in Lichfield society: " Mr. Day looked the philosopher. Powder and fine clothes were, at that time, the appendages of gentlemen. Mr. Day wore not either. He was tall and stooped in the shoulders, full made, but not corpulent; and in his meditative and melancholy air a degree of awkwardness and dignity were blended. We found his features interesting and agreeable amidst the traces of a severe smallpox. There was a sort of weight upon the lids of his large hazel eyes; yet when he declaimed . . . very expressive were the energies gleaming from them beneath the shade of sable hair, which, Adam-like, curled about his brows." His like-ness at that time has been pictorially transmitted to posterity by Wright of Derby, and posterity should be grateful to Anna Seward for her description of the portrait: " Drawn as in the open air, the surrounding sky is tempestuous, lurid and dark. He stands leaning his left arm against a column inscribed to Hampden. Mr. Day looks upward, as enthusiastically meditating on the contents of a book, held in his dropped right hand. The open leaf is the oration of that virtuous patriot in the senate, against the grant of ship-money, demanded by King Charles the first. A flash of lightning plays in Mr. Day's hair, and illumines the contents of the volume.''

Sabrina was now a beautiful girl of thirteen. '' Her countenance,'' says Edgeworth, '' was engaging. She had fine auburn hair, that hung in natural ringlets on her neck; a beauty which was then more striking, because other people wore enormous quantities of powder and pomatum. Her long eyelashes, and eyes expressive of sweetness, interested all who saw her, and the uncommon melody of her voice made a favourable impression upon every person to whom she spoke. I was curious to see how my friend's philosophic romance would end.''

No one in Lichfield thought any the worse of Day for his plan of educating a girl for the responsibilities of wifehood. In fact the ladies of the place were singularly interested in the experiment, and Sabrina was received by the Sewards at the bishop's palace, which meant that she was received everywhere. Day had now reached an advanced stage in his scheme of education, and, shortly after his arrival at Lichfield, he began to practise a method of Higher Education which he was convinced would prove salutary to the soul of Sabrina.

The older he had grown the more powerfully had he been impressed by the doctrines and examples of the Stoics, and it struck him that here was a heaven-sent opportunity of putting his theories into practice. In order to bring up his offspring in the way they should go, Sabrina would have to teach them to suffer ills uncomplainingly and endure hardships with fortitude. How could she do this unless she set them an example, unless she displayed the virtues she wished them to acquire? It was clear, then, that her powers of endurance must be tested. Several methods of testing them occurred to Day. Two were adopted and promptly put into practice.

There were, he decided, two classes of cowards—those who shrank from immediate physical pain, and those who were terrified by the apprehension of danger. His methods were carefully selected to prove complete immunity from cowardice in both forms, should the patient survive the ordeal. First, he believed that the dropping of melted sealing-wax on the neck and arms of Sabrina would, if she treated it as an ordinary occurrence, definitely signify her indifference to immediate physical pain. He tried it, but was disagreeably surprised to note that, as the wax sizzled and hardened on her flesh, she so far forgot herself as to scream.

But there was still hope. A woman who could not endure acute suffering, because of some inherited effeminacy, might yet be stoical under the threat of mortal danger. He informed her therefore that he had loaded his pistol and begged her to have sufficient faith in the accuracy of his aim, and his proved affection for herself, not to jump when he fired a bullet into her petticoats. Taking a careful aim at her legs, he then fired off a blank cartridge, and was shocked to observe that she not only jumped but emitted a howl of terror. He was not, however, callous enough to give her up in despair at the first failure. He wanted her to have every possible chance of gaining his good opinion; so he went on blazing away hopefully at her skirts. But, try as he might, the wretched girl failed to justify her claim to his "compassion and indulgence," and he was mortified beyond measure when, at every repetition of the explosion, she continued to show traces of discomposure. In the hope that hardening would come with time, he repeated these experiments, with others of a similar nature, at intervals during his year's residence at Lichfield; but Sabrina never really got used to them, and continually vexed him with her querulous complaints.

At length his patience gave way. Her commonplace reactions to danger and pain convinced him that there was nothing noble, nothing heroic, in her character; and he decided that she was not worthy to be the mother of his children. "His trust in the power of education faltered," Miss Seward informs us, "his aversion to modern elegance subsided." A euphemistic way of saying that Day had fallen in love with someone else. Sabrina was dismissed to a boarding-school in Sutton-Coldfield, and Day turned his attention to Honora Sneyd. This lady lived with the Sewards and was adored by all of them. Her father had put her under their care at the death of her mother, and she was treated at the bishop's palace as one of the family. Edgeworth, who was spending a few weeks with Day, fell in love with Honora on the spot, and all his friends "were unanimous in their approbation of the lady." But Edgeworth was a married man and a man of honour, so the moment Day "became sensible of Honora's charms" he went home to his wife and family.

Day, at first, had not liked Honora. She danced too well, she was too fashionable, and her arms were not sufficiently round and white to please him. Also, it is conceivable that she had treated him to a few ironical comments on the pistol-and-sealing-wax treatment. Be that as it may, his "intentions with regard to Sabrina began to change" and "his mind turned toward Miss Honora Sneyd." Day knew of Edgeworth's feelings and wrote to him pointing out "the folly and meanness of indulging a hopeless passion" and asking whether he had "sufficient strength of mind totally to subdue love that cannot be indulged compatibly with peace, or honour, or virtue?"

Edgeworth gave an immediate proof of his strength of mind. He took his wife and family to Lichfield, so as to be "in the company of the dangerous object," and stayed there with Day for some time. Honora and Thomas were now always about together and it seemed to Edgeworth that "nothing was wanting but a declaration on his part and compliance on the part of the lady." Then one morning Day, "in a very solemn manner," presented Edgeworth with a heavy packet and begged him to deliver it into the hands of Honora Sneyd. "It is," said Day, "a proposal of marriage. It contains the sum of many conversations that have passed between us. I am satisfied that, if the plan of life I have here laid down meets her approbation, we shall be perfectly happy. Honora Sneyd is so reasonable, so perfectly sincere, and so much to be relied on, that if once she resolves to live a calm, secluded life, she will never wish to return to more gay or splendid scenes. If she once turn away from public admiration, she will never look back again with regret."

Edgeworth handed the packet to Honora, who told him to come for an answer the following morning. In the interval Day "expressed extreme anxiety." The answer was duly received by Edgeworth and delivered to Day. "It was" (to quote Edgeworth) "a clear dispassionate view of the rights of women. Miss Honora Sneyd would not admit the unqualified control of a husband over all her actions; she did not feel that seclusion from society was indispensably necessary to preserve female virtue or to secure domestic happiness." In conclusion, "she would not change her present mode of life, with which she had no reason to be dissatisfied, for any dark and untried system that could be proposed to her."

The effect of the letter on Day was instantaneous and disastrous. He collapsed, and was seriously ill with a high fever for several days. Dr. Darwin ordered him to be bled, and incidentally gave him a good sound talking-to. It is difficult to say what might have happened to Thomas if, when he was up and about again, someone had not arrived on the scene and distracted his attention from Honora. This was Honora's sister, Elizabeth, who now came with her father to live in Lichfield. She danced poorly, which pleased Mr. Day. She took no pleasure in dancing, which delighted Mr. Day. She never argued, which charmed Mr. Day. She listened to him with admiration in her looks and attention in her attitude while he discoursed at large on all the subjects that lay near to his heart, which completely captured Mr. Day.

Nevertheless, there was one fly in the ointment. She did not like his manners, and told him so. She went further. She told him that it ill became him to scoff at accomplishments to which he could not lay claim. Though the social talents he affected to despise might be trivial and frivolous, he was the last man who should abuse them, since he had been incapable of acquiring them. This touched him on the raw, and he decided to acquire social polish in order that he might abuse it with impunity. It so happened that his friend Edgeworth had just resolved on flight from the seductive charms of Honora, and "the danger, the criminality of such an attachment." They determined therefore to visit France together. But before he left Elizabeth Sneyd, Day extracted a promise from her that she should not go to London, Bath, or any public place of amusement, during his absence, and that she should "prosecute an excellent course of reading" while he was bruising himself in continental ball-rooms.

Reasonably reassured on all these points, Day proceeded to Lyons in the company of Edgeworth. "Here," says Edgeworth, "Mr. Day put himself to every species of torture, ordinary and extraordinary, to compel his anti-gallican limbs, in spite of their natural rigidity, to dance, and fence, and manage the *great horse*. To perform his promise to Miss E. Sneyd honourably, he gave up seven or eight hours of the day to these exercises, for which he had not the slightest taste, and for which, except horsemanship, he manifested the most sovereign contempt. It was astonishing to behold the energy with which he persevered in these pursuits. I have seen him stand between two boards, which reached from the ground higher than his knees: these boards were adjusted with screws, so as barely to permit him to bend his knees, and to rise up and sink down. By these means M. Huise proposed to force Mr. Day's knees outward; but his screwing was in vain. He succeeded in torturing his patient; but original formation and inveterate habit resisted all his endeavours at personal improvement. I could not help pitying my philosophic friend, pent up in durance vile for hours together, with his feet in the stocks, a book in his hand, and contempt in his heart."

After several months spent in the acquirement of social polish, Day returned to England to claim, as the reward of his labours, the hand of Miss Elizabeth Sneyd. Alas! Lichfield laughed at him. Miss Seward noted that the endeavours he made to carry himself well were more ungraceful than his natural stoop and unfashionable air. " The studied bow on entrance, the suddenly recollected *assumption* of attitude, prompted the risible instead of the admiring sensation; neither was the showy dress, in which he came back to his fair one, a jot more becoming." As for Elizabeth Sneyd, she frankly admitted that Thomas Day, blackguard (as he used to style himself), appealed to her more than Thomas Day, gentleman. All the exertions he had made, all the pains he had taken to improve the outer man, were thrown away. " Notwithstanding his great and good qualities, she could not give him her heart." Tragic words! Tragic, but true. Both heroism and adoration are necessary qualities in a woman who proposes to marry one who prompts " the risible instead of the admiring sensation," and Thomas never inspired those qualities in Elizabeth.

Day wore a gloomy expression for the correct number of weeks, months, or years, and went back to plain clothing, bad manners, good principles, and philosophy. It is to his credit that when, in due time, Edgeworth married first Honora, and afterwards Elizabeth Sneyd, their friendship remained unimpaired. " With what pleasure," wrote Day when his friend married Honora, " shall I, when I meet you again, contemplate that happiness which you say you so fully possess! Such sights are sometimes necessary to reconcile me to the mass of misery I see around me." Day was always more than conscious of the mass of misery around him, and spent a great deal of his yearly income in trying to alleviate it.

From 1773 onwards Day lived in the Temple, though he made frequent excursions to various parts of England. Much of his time was spent in the company of Dr. Small, who contrived to make him a little less idealistic in outlook and a little more practical in his attitude towards life. Though unknown to posterity, Small gained an enormous ascendancy over the minds of most of his friends, and as many of these were drawn from the Darwin circle—Watt, Boulton, Priestley, etc.—it is clear that he was a personality of note. His influence over Day—all for the good—was extraordinary. Though he never succeeded in making Day a reasonable being, he did succeed in making him a reasoning being, which was a pretty considerable feather in his cap. Among other things he decided that something had to be done about Day's marriage. He felt sure that his friend's happiness largely depended upon a suitable wife, a sturdy family, and a settled home; so he set about the business of finding Day the right kind of domestic partner. Quite accidentally, he came across a lady—Miss Milnes, of Wakefield, in Yorkshire—who in his opinion would fulfil all the vital requirements, who was capable of appreciating the merits of his friend and of treating the defects of his manners and appearance as trifles beneath her notice. Dr. Small was on the point of revealing his "find" to Day, when the latter once more turned his attention to Sabrina.

She was by this time a very attractive young lady, and, after his recent misfortunes with the Sneyd family, Day decided to give her a final chance. Once more he tried to enlarge her understanding and "mould her mind and disposition to his own views and pursuits." He gave her to understand that the future Mrs. Day "must be content to live in perfect retirement, to give up her tastes for his, to discuss every subject of every day's occurrence with logical accuracy, to be totally indifferent to all the luxuries and some of the comforts of opulent life." In return for these sacrifices which, considered rationally, were more in the nature of thanksgivings, Edgeworth states that the future Mrs. Day "would find herself united to a man of undeviating morality, sound sense, much knowledge, and much celebrity; a companion never deficient in instructive or agreeable conversation, of great good nature, of unbounded generosity; a philanthropist in the most extensive and most exalted sense of the word: in short, a man who would put it in her power to do good to everybody beneath her, provided she could scorn the silly fashions of those above her."

We have it on the authority of Edgeworth that Sabrina loved Thomas, but that she was too young and too artless to attach much importance to his taste in female dress. There can be little doubt that, at this moment, he was on the point of marrying her. Edgeworth was obviously amazed at his ability to resist a girl who was so "peculiarly pleasing to him in her person." But alas! Sabrina again failed to come up to the scratch. And this time it was neither burning sealing-wax nor the ignition of gunpowder at close quarters that cost her the love of her guardian. Already, under Dr. Small's tuition, he had begun to realize that there were many forms of courage and that the ability to suppress a shriek under disquieting circumstances was not necessarily a proof of the highest form. No; it would be enough now if he could feel sure that Sabrina really and truly loved him. The test he made of her affection was a simple one. Anyone could have passed it with flying colours. It required no physical hardihood, no mental stress, no moral pluck. It required merely an unselfish devotion to Thomas.

In leaving Sabrina at the house of a friend, he told her that he was dissatisfied with certain items of her apparel. She had even dared to look fashionable under his very nose. Certain sleeves she wore . . . well, the less said about them the better. And a kerchief . . . yes, he had spoken to her before about the kerchief. It was very wrong of her to go against his wishes. She must prove her love by mending her ways. In short, during his absence, she must dress . . . he explained how she must dress. But the moment his back was turned, fashion reasserted itself, and his friend had to inform him that she had failed to carry out his instructions. Thereupon Day cast her from him, allowed her £50 a year, and never saw her again except in the presence of witnesses.

Ironic fate had not yet finished with Sabrina. Day's friend, Mr. Bicknel, who had advised him to select Sabrina from among the "prattling inmates" of Shrewsbury Foundling Hospital, had been living the gay life of eighteenth-century bachelordom. "The evidence you bring of Mr. Bicknel's bachelor voluptuousness is irresistibly strong," wrote Anna Seward to a friend some time after Bicknel's death: "I suppose Mr. Day knew it not, or, with his general abhorrence of sensuality, he had spared to mention him with so much esteem—but Lord! what a pale, maidenish-looking animal for a voluptuary!—so reserved as were his manners!—and his countenance!—a very tablet, upon which the ten commandments seemed written." This gentleman, then, having sown a vast quantity of wild oats, began at last to feel the effects of his protracted debauchery. "Considering that it would be a comfort to secure a companion for middle life, and a friend, perhaps a nurse, for his declining years, he determined to marry." This touching testimony is given by Edgeworth's daughter, Maria. He made inquiries, learned that Sabrina was living, unmarried, and a virgin; saw her, fell desperately in love with her, and proposed marriage. Sabrina would not marry without Mr. Day's consent, and asked him for it. Day's reply suggests that he was not wholly ignorant of the budding bride-groom's qualifications: "I do not refuse my *consent* to your marrying Mr. Bicknel," said he, "but remember you have not asked my *advice*." They married, begat two boys, and were happy. But Mr. Bicknel now had to reap what he had sown; a paralytic stroke finished him off, and poor Sabrina had to rear her children on charity and hard work. As Anna said, it was "hard to be dependent upon the bounty of friends, especially after having married rather from discretion than from choice."

Meanwhile, Dr. Small announced his discovery of Miss Milnes to his friend Day. He explained that her charity and benevolence were known throughout York-shire; he produced letters which proved the superiority of her understanding; and he declared that from every point of view she seemed an ideal wife for Day.

"But," said Day, "has she white and large arms?"

"She has," said Dr. Small.

"Does she wear long petticoats?"

"Uncommonly long."

"I hope she is tall, and strong, and healthy."

"Remarkably little, and not robust," replied the honest doctor. Day was about to raise an objection, but Small raised a hand and leisurely enumerated the points in the lady's favour: " Can you possibly expect that a woman of charming temper, benevolent mind, and cultivated understanding, with a distinguished character, with views of life congenial with your own, with an agreeable person and a large fortune, should be formed exactly according to a picture that exists in your imagination? This lady is two or three and twenty, has had twenty admirers; some of them admirers of herself, some, perhaps, of her fortune; yet, in spite of all these admirers and lovers, she is disengaged. If you are not satisfied, determine at once never to marry."

" My dear doctor," rejoined Day, " the only serious objection which I have to Miss Milnes is her large fortune. It was always my wish to give to any woman whom I married the most unequivocal proof of my attachment to herself by despising her fortune."

" Well, my dear friend," said the doctor, " what prevents you from despising the fortune and taking the lady?"

Mr. Day went into Yorkshire, was charmed with Miss Milnes, and commenced a courtship which any other man would have concluded in a few months. The lady loved and admired him. He loved and admired the lady. But " there were a thousand small preliminaries to be adjusted. . . . There was no subject of opinion or speculation which he did not, previously to his marriage, discuss with his intended bride." After several years spent in conversation and correspondence over the many knotty points that arose during their intercourse, and the innumerable subjects, from poetry to poverty, on which it was desirable they should agree, they married. But that did not prevent them from talking; they went on discussing politics and metaphysics and such-like themes until their contract was terminated by death.

Day now decided to put his scheme for connubial happiness into practice. He refused to live near any of his friends, lest their opinions on the marriage question should influence his wife. He took lodgings in Hampstead, where they lived a life of Spartan seclusion. Mr. and Mrs. Edgeworth went to visit them one day in mid-winter, and though the snow was thick on the ground, and Mrs. Day had a particularly delicate constitution, they were walking about the heath in glorious indifference to the elements.

A little later Day bought a house and small estate called Stapleford-Abbot, near Abridge, in Essex. Here his wife was made to realize that she had not married him for the mere fun of the thing. She was allowed no servant, no carriage, no luxury of any sort. He put a stop to all correspondence between her and her family. She sang and played well, but music, in the opinion of Thomas, was trivial, so she had to give up her harpsichord and banish her music-books. "We have no right to luxuries," said Thomas, "while the poor want bread." Mrs. Day might have complained that, by denying themselves music, they were not helping the poor to bear their poverty. But on a point of discipline she never argued with her husband; being a good and devoted wife, she just did as she was told. He made frequent experiments on her temper and her love, the nature of which has not been revealed to us, though we know enough of him to hazard a few guesses. "Over these," says Anna Seward, "she often wept, but never repined."

The house Day had bought was not large enough for them, so he decided to add to it. He got a book on architecture, which he read and re-read for several weeks before commencing operations. Then he issued a number of orders to builders and promptly buried himself in a treatise written by some French agriculturist which proved that any soil could be rendered fertile if one went on ploughing it long enough. While he was in the middle of this, he was continually being pestered by the builders for such things as sills, lintels, doors, and window-cases, which he had forgotten to order. A carpenter was hastily sent for and set to work; but the business of building was already beginning to get on his nerves. The long discussions he liked to have with his wife were interrupted at awkward moments; the noises of the workmen prevented their close application to books when in the house; and weeks after he had disposed of architecture—indeed, when he had nearly completed his study of agriculture—the masons would worry him with absurd questions about the position of a window in a wall. One day, while deep in the French treatise on the potential fertility of soil, a workman poked his head round the door and asked where he would have the window of the new room on the first floor, which was to be Mrs. Day's dressing-room. Absorbed for the moment in the subject of soil, Day gravely inquired whether the wall might not be built first and a place for the window cut out afterwards? The fellow stared at Day in amazement, admitted that such a thing was possible, but said that the usual method was to allow for the windows during the process of building the wall. Day saw no particular reason for following the usual course and ordered the wall to be built without an opening for a window. For several years Mrs. Day had to dress by candle-light.

Eventually Day bought another house and estate at Anningley, near Chertsey—"one of the most unprofitable farms in England," he called it—where he tried upon a large scale several of those doubtful agricultural processes which he had read about in books, and which relieved him of a considerable part of his fortune. He was always very kind to the poor and ran his farm more as a philanthropic institution than as a paying concern. He paid his labourers better wages in the winter than in the summer, because they wanted "more comforts at this severe season of the year." And, naturally, he was much disliked by the surrounding farmers, who were opposed to the principle of philanthropic farming.

His idealistic outlook on life had become considerably modified with time and he now regarded mankind, and most of his acquaintance, with a sort of contemptuous toleration. Nevertheless, in these later years, he worked and spoke for the extension of the franchise, never troubling to explain why people who in his opinion were worthless should not be voteless. Attempts were made to draw him into party controversy, but he refused to be drawn. His attitude to the politicians of his time was clearly illustrated by a remark he made in a letter to one of them: "I cannot conceive why a set of men who are already in possession of all their ambition can wish, may not as well consult the true interest of the country as basely endeavour to destroy it." Other people besides Day have been in the same quandary. He was one of the first 'humanitarians,' was violently opposed to slavery, which he lamented in poetry and denounced in prose; and in a number of pamphlets he asked America what right she had to fight for freedom when at the same time she kept her negroes in bondage.

Though scarcely orthodox in his religious beliefs, he would ask the labourers to his house on Sundays and impart moral instruction. All his life he was rigidly independent in spirit and utterly indifferent to the effect his behaviour had on the outside world. For example, he would sometimes prescribe a medicine for a friend, and persist in his prescription against all the objurgations of the doctors in the neighbourhood. In the last year of his life he took on a case where the patient was hovering between life and death, and cured him in the very teeth of the faculty and in spite of their gravest warnings. He always questioned authority and tradition. The fact that a certain thing was done merely because it was the thing to do annoyed him and aroused his antagonism. His mother was horrified when she found him, during a serious attack of ague, sitting up in bed and placidly demolishing a plateful of hashed goose. And his wife, whose tender body probably required tender treatment, was never allowed to be ill. If she made the slightest reference to her health, she was instantly hustled out of the house and walked off her legs.

His death was due to a theory, which he held with the utmost tenacity, that animals could be controlled by kindness. Whenever a horse was unruly or vicious, it was due, he said, to ill-usage from man. He endeavoured therefore to train a horse for himself by gentle means. On 28 September, 1789, he mounted it and started off on a visit to his mother. But the animal had not been broken in and shied at something near Wargrave. It plunged fiercely, would not respond to kindness, and Day was flung from the saddle on to his head. He died almost at once. His wife survived him for two years. Her husband's friends declared that she died of a broken heart. But if we are to believe Anna Seward, who says that she never afterwards saw the sun but lay all day in bed with the curtains drawn, it is possible that Thomas would have ascribed her death to lack of exercise.

Thus perished, at the early age of forty-one, a man who, in the words of Blackman, had done his best " to make the world more heavenly and man more Godlike." Anna Seward's view of his ideals was not quite the same as Blackman's. In a letter written to the *General Evening Post* a fortnight after his death, she said:

. . . But let him be spoken of as he was, for truth is better than indiscriminate eulogium. Mr. Day, with very first-rate abilities, was a splenetic, capricious, yet bountiful misanthropist. He bestowed nearly the whole of his ample fortune in relieving the necessities of the poor ; frequently, however, declaring his conviction that there were few in the large number he fed who would not cut his throat the next hour, if their interest could prompt the act, and their lives be safe in its commission. He took pride in avowing his abhorrence of the luxuries and disdain of even the decencies of life ; and in his person he was generally slovenly, even to squalidness. On being asked by one of his friends why he chose the lonely and unpleasant situation in which he lived, he replied that the sole reason of that choice was—its being out of the stink of human society. . . .

CHAPTER VI

THE GREAT POTTER

DAY, it appears, was fonder of Darwin than of anyone except Edgeworth and Small. And here we stumble across a curious fact: the doctor was nearly everyone's second-best friend. Considering the quality of his friends, this is his highest tribute. He was far too busy to cultivate a single intimate friendship; yet, after their own bosom friends, every member of his circle turned instinctively to him for help, advice, or solace in their trouble. And they did not turn in vain.

Watt and Boulton worked together and could develop their friendship both in and out of business. But each looked upon Darwin as the best fellow in the world except the other. Edgeworth and Day, even when they were not living together, were in constant communion with one another. The main subject of their talk, after philosophy, was Dr. Darwin, their next-best friend. James Keir was the doctor's lifelong friend and probably held him first in his affection, or at least bracketed him with Day. There is a revealing passage in one of his letters to the doctor: " Mr. Boulton set out this day on a journey to Cornwall, where he will probably remain three weeks. He has been so much absent from home, and when at home in such a whirlpool of business, that there has scarcely been even a Sunday which could be devoted to *Philosophy and Doctor Darwin.* I long much to see you. . . ."

Then there was Josiah Wedgwood, the great potter, whose partner, Thomas Bentley, was his friend-of-friends. But the doctor came next, and, after Bentley's death, took his place in the affection of Josiah.

Josiah Wedgwood, the youngest of a large family, was born in 1730. He came of a family of potters; but his father died when he was young and he had to start life at the bottom of the ladder. In those days the disease of smallpox ravaged the country periodically, and Josiah, who caught it badly, probably owed his survival to the fact that there was no doctor in the neighbourhood; for then, even more than now, doctors were worse than useless in epidemics. The disease left him permanently weakened and subject to frequent illnesses; it also affected his leg, which, in course of time, and after several subsidiary accidents, had to be amputated.

When he became an apprentice, his indenture contained this clause: " Cards, dice, or any other unlawful games he shall not play; taverns or ale-houses he shall not haunt or frequent; fornication he shall not commit; matrimony he shall not contract." His biographer expresses the belief that the retention of this clause " shows distinctly that most worthy influences were in operation around the boy." But it is far more likely that the clause was retained simply because it was never cut out. One may assume that the master-potters had once been apprentices themselves.

However that may be, the clause was quite unnecessary in the case of Josiah. He was a strictly righteous, sober, and chaste young man, who studied chemistry in his spare time. Gradually he worked himself into a position of independence, and by the time he had become a master of his art he was able to start his own pot-work. "Though subsequently disused," his biographer tells us, " he always retained his marvellous skill . . . so that at the distance of forty years he could still give a practical example to his throwers, and by merely poising a newly-thrown vessel in his left hand, he would tell at a glance its defects or beauties. If it failed even minutely in its geometrical proportions, he would, before his leg was taken off, break it up with the stick which he then always carried, remarking as he did so, ' This won't do for Josiah Wedgwood.'"

Wedgwood was that strange combination—a man of business who was also and always a human being. Darwin said of him: " I never knew an instance of a man raising himself to such opulence and distinction who excited so little envy. . . . He was free from the failing which frequently attends easily-acquired riches of neglecting his poor relations." He hated accounts and lost thousands by not attending to that part of his business. Sometimes he would begin to enter up his expenses in a pocket-book, but after a while the figures would give way to notes on forms, colours, and mixtures. He never prosecuted people who owed him money, and whenever it came to his knowledge that his subordinates had done so, he instantly paid all the costs himself and enlarged the defaulter. In spite of this he died worth half a million of money, in those days a gigantic fortune.

Simplicity, modesty, and industry were his strongest characteristics. He simply could not be idle. He rose with the sun in the summer and before it was light in the winter, and was usually busy in his works before his men arrived. There was an entire harmony between his moral and intellectual faculties, which accounts no doubt for the physical courage and unruffled energy he displayed throughout life. Nothing in his career reveals him to us so clearly as the way he bore the loss of his leg. It became a hindrance to his work, so he resolved to have it cut off before the opening of his factory at Etruria, when a dead limb would more than ever be an encumbrance to him. In those days there was no anæsthetic, and operations were performed with much of the callousness and crudeness of the Middle Ages. Yet when the time came he refused all assistance, refused even to have the operation hidden from his view, but sat down calmly in his chair and contemplated the hacking and sawing without a groan.

Those were Spartan days. His trusted and devoted servant, Peter Swift, treated the occurrence with equal composure. Appended to an invoice on Wedgwood's London house for " piggins, cream pots, salts," etc., we read this:

Burslem, 28th May, 1768.

Sir, Your favour of the 26th is just come to hand, but can make no reply to the contents. Mr. Wedgwood has this day had his leg taken of, & is as well as can be expected after such an execution. The revd. Mr. Horne's Goods are packed, and one Crate for the warehouse, the particulars of which I shall insert at foot, or as much as time will permitt. Mr. Chester's Goods will be delivered on Thursday next. I am, &c. . . . PETER SWIFT.

Wedgwood probably owed his introduction to Darwin to the fact that he was constantly ill. We do not, however, catch our first glimpse of the doctor in the Wedgwood correspondence until 1765, when they are already old friends, and the subject under discussion is not medical.

Darwin was by this time a man of considerable note throughout the Midlands. His practice was enormous. It was the general opinion that he had revolutionized the art of the physician. He founded the methods he used for the recovery of his patients upon the varying necessities of the case, utterly discarding the orthodox medicines which were invariably prescribed for definite diseases without reference to individual reactions. With all the daring of genius he had introduced new medicines and used old ones in cases that staggered his timid professional brethren. "To him," we are told, "routine was nothing, the necessities and circumstances of the case before him everything; and thus, by the simple observation of facts, or by meditation on them, he was the true servant and interpreter of nature."

Later on we shall see him at work; and though we may smile at his use of depletion, both by purgatives and bleeding, we must remember that inflammatory diseases were then far more severe and infinitely more common than they are now, and that in the majority of cases he saved the lives of his patients.

In spite of his practice, which made him spend the greater number of his days and nights in his carriage, he yet found time for poetry, science, philosophy, the arts, a large correspondence, innumerable mechanical experiments and inventions, and commercial development. It is in connection with the Trent and Mersey navigation scheme that we first meet him with Wedgwood. The great potter was naturally interested in roads and canals; the development of his business depended upon the improvement of the first and the introduction of the second. So we find him putting all his energy into the scheme for linking the Mersey to the Trent by a canal and getting his friends interested.

Darwin at once gave him all the help he could. There was considerable opposition to the scheme, from rival interests and mere conservatism, and it was necessary to issue a pamphlet and a plan to the public. Darwin was ever ready to help with advice and criticism and by quietly influencing some of the leading obstructionists who happened to be his patients, such as Earl Ferrers, the Earl of Uxbridge, and others, all of whom had a financial interest in opposing the scheme.

The pamphlet was being prepared by Bentley, and Darwin supplied him with a lot of valuable information, eventually settling the vexed question of the dedication. But it was not all easy going. The doctor's satirical manner of writing caused occasional heart-burnings among the enthusiasts, and Wedgwood had to smooth things over. He knew the doctor pretty thoroughly and never took offence at the sarcastic sallies which were as characteristic of him as his stammer and just as superficial.

The doctor thought Bentley's style in the pamphlet "too flat and tame." Wedgwood saved the situation by reminding Bentley that the doctor was a poetical genius and therefore liked high-sounding phrases. Later, when Darwin's dedication to the Queen was superseded by one to the Parliament from the pen of Bentley, the doctor wrote: "Nobody writes Grace and Rt. Honourable but Taylors and such-like folks." Wedgwood, scenting danger, instantly gave Bentley *carte blanche* to do as he pleased. Later still, the doctor addressed himself to Bentley at some length. Wedgwood heard of it, and promptly forestalled any possible misunderstanding by laughing it off. Thus:

"I doubt not you have received my letter from Uttoxeter and Derby—and a long, critical and explanatory letter from our ingenious and poetical friend Doctor Darwin, which I doubt not (if it be such as he generally favours his friends with) hath afforded you entertainment and shook your diaphragm for you, whatever it may have done respecting your pamphlet on Navigation."

In the midst of all this Wedgwood had one of his recurrent attacks of illness. The doctor rushed to Burslem, examined him carefully, and set his mind at rest over any little misunderstandings that may have occurred between himself and Bentley. "I am got pretty well," writes Wedgwood to his friend, "but not perfectly recovered. Dr. Darwin, who stop'd all

night with me at Burslem last week, hath prescribed
something for me which he says will strengthen the
machinery and set it all to rights again. The Dr.
acknowledg'd he had wrote you two or three very rude
letters and said you had drub'd him genteely in return,
which he seem'd to take very cordially and to be very
well pleas'd with his treatment.''

Eventually the pamphlet was published. A subscrip-
tion was started to defray the costs of pushing the
necessary Bill through Parliament; and after prolonged
negotiation and strife, and the usual waste of time and
money, the Bill was passed in the spring of 1766.
Wedgwood received universal congratulations, and an
interesting letter from Darwin, who tells him that a
certain French nobleman, Count de Lauraguais, '' has
been at Birmingham and offer'd ye Secret of making
ye finest old China, as cheap as your Pots. He says
ye materials are in England. That ye Secret has cost
£16,000, y^t He will sell it for £2000. . . . He is a
Man of Science, dislikes his own Country, was six
months in ye Bastile for speaking against ye Government—loves everything English. . . . But I suspect
his Scientific Passion is stronger than perfect Sanity.
. . . I congratulate you on ye Success of your Act of
Parliament. Adieu.'' Darwin never missed an opportunity of telling his friends about anything he came
across that might affect or interest them. . . .

Needless to say, the moment Wedgwood bought a
large property for his new house and works, Darwin
was consulted. Suggestions and plans for the laying-
out of the estate poured from him. Wedgwood,

though self-reliant and self-possessed to an extra-ordinary degree, never tired of seeking Darwin's advice, and usually took it. Knowing the doctor's love of classical allusion, he might have hesitated before asking him to christen the place; but the moment Darwin suggested "Etruria," he accepted the name without demur—and Etruria it became. He even confided his greatest chemical secrets to the doctor, who shared them with Mrs. Wedgwood and Bentley.

Darwin was always thinking of something useful for his friend, and in 1768 he wrote to say that he was constructing a windmill "to grind colours (if it should happen to grind anything) for our intended ornamental works at Etruria." (Note that "our.") Wedgwood treated the thing as a joke until he went to Lichfield, when a personal inspection of the windmill aroused his interest and respect. Indeed, if it had not been for the doctor, he would have set it up at once. But the doctor's honesty, generosity, and foresight prevented this. James Watt was, at this very moment, experimenting with his steam-engine, and had imparted the plan of his improvements to Darwin under a pledge of secrecy. The doctor, without breaking trust, warned Wedgwood to do nothing in a hurry:

I should long ago have wrote to you, but waited to learn in what forwardness Mr. Watt's Fire-Engine was in. He has taken a Partner, and I can make no conjecture how soon you may be accommodated by Him with a Power so much more convenient than that of Wind. I will make packing Boxes & send you my model, y^t you may consult the In-genious. I am of opinion it will be a powerful and convenient Windmill, but would recommend steam to you if you can wait awhile, as it will on many Accounts be preferable I believe for all Purposes.

A little later he writes:

Your windmill sleeps at my house, but shall be sent you, if you wish it, but I should advise you to wait the Wheel-Fire-Engine, which goes on slowly.

Ten years after, with the assistance of Watt and Edgeworth, the doctor's windmill was set up at Etruria. . . .

Darwin liked all his friends to be the friends of his friends. James Keir, called by Watt "a mighty chemist and a very agreeable man," was quickly initiated into the Wedgwood circle. Darwin introduced him thus:

Dear Wedgwood,

I have the pleasure to introduce to your acquaintance Captain James Keir, an old Friend of mine, a successful cultivator of both Arts and Arms. He begs the Favour of seeing your elegant manufactory & hopes to meet our common Friend, the Philosopher, Mr. Whitehurst at your House. The Civilities you shew Capt. Keir will be received by Dear Sir your affectt. humble Sert., E. Darwin.

After the visit Darwin writes to Wedgwood:

Capt. Keir is at present at Birmingham. He desired I would say all the fine Things I could think of to thank Mrs. Wedgwood for the Trouble He gave her ; of whom indeed he speaks very highly, & was much entertained with your manufactory.

From this time the acquaintance ripened and Wedgwood frequently met Keir at the house of Dr. Small in Birmingham, or at Soho, where for a time Keir was managing Boulton's works. . . .

Brindley, the famous engineer who had made the Trent and Mersey Canal, died in 1772. Though he had been ill for seven years, no doctor had been able to discover that he was dying of diabetes until Darwin came along. It was then too late to do anything but write his epitaph:

Dear Wedgwood,

I did not return soon enough out of Derbyshire to answer your letter by yesterday's post. Your second letter gave me great consolation about Mrs. Wedgwood, but gave me most sincere grief about Mr. Brindley, whom I have always esteemed to be a great genius, and whose loss is truly a public one. I don't believe he has left his equal. I think the various Navigations should erect him a monument in Westminster Abbey, and hope you will at the proper time give them this hint.

Mr. Stanier sent me no account of him, except of his death, though I so much desired it, since if I had understood that he got worse, nothing should have hindered me from seeing him again. If Mr. Henshaw took any Journal of his illness or other circumstances after I saw him, *I wish you would ask him for it and enclose it to me.* And any circumstances that you recollect of his life should be wrote down, and I will some time digest them into an Eulogium. These men should not die ; this Nature denies ; but their Memories are above her Malice. Enough !

Wedgwood's friendship for Darwin was further strengthened by the fact that the doctor had saved Mrs. Wedgwood's life over and over again. During 1772 and 1773 she was extremely ill and for weeks together her life was despaired of. The doctor spent every minute he could snatch from his multifarious duties at her bedside. To his care, no less than to his skill, Wedgwood owed her preservation. When she got better the doctor wanted to rush her off to Buxton, but as her husband had business to transact in Bath, they went there instead. Bath did not agree with her and they returned home. The doctor's genius and diligence were now called on again. Her existence hung upon a thread. The illness was complicated by "a crisis in her maternal situation," which left her in such a deplorable state of weakness that the doctor had to sit up with her all night. For days she lay nearer death than life, and her relations were horrified by the doctor's prescriptions. He told Wedgwood to give her ripe plums and cider, which her nurses thought equivalent to poison. Convalescence came slowly, but was followed by a fearful relapse. Wedgwood was in terrible distress, but he had faith in the doctor, and at last he was rewarded. She recovered gradually, and Darwin took her to Lichfield, where under his constant care her health was restored.

During these early years of their friendship the Darwin family often went to stay with the Wedgwoods and the Wedgwoods with the Darwins. Wedgwood had listened to the doctor's advanced views on education and profited by them. If a boy is going to be engaged in trade, said the doctor, Latin will be useless to him: let him learn French. The great potter's scientific tastes were also developed and broadened under the doctor's influence; and in the course of their talks and correspondence on chemistry Darwin, ever in the vanguard of thought, seems to have apprehended the atomic theory which was afterwards associated with the name of Dalton. Though full of ideas, Wedgwood had not of course the scientific mind of Darwin, and a passage in one of the doctor's letters tells as much:

I admire the way in which you support your new theory of freezing steam. You say " Will not vapour freeze with a less degree of cold than water in the mass ? instances hoar-frost &c." Now this same *et caetera*, my dear friend, seems to me to be a gentleman of such consequence to your theory, that I wish he would unfold himself a little more.

Children's bodies, no less than their minds, were roughly treated in the eighteenth century. When one of Wedgwood's babies suffered convulsions, produced by teething, she lost the use of her limbs and sight. "The usual nostrums for this disease," we are assured, " were burnt blood, a baked raven, with a long et-cetera." But Darwin laughed them all to scorn and instructed Wedgwood to chafe the child's limbs, lance her gums, hold her in the bath and electrify her. Though the child recovered the use of her limbs and sight, one is not surprised to learn that she died in infancy; and one cannot help wondering whether, on the whole, she would not have preferred the burnt blood, the baked raven, and possibly even the etcetera. . . .

In 1780 Thomas Bentley, Wedgwood's partner and bosom friend, died. Darwin did his best to administer comfort:

Your letter communicating to me the death of your friend, and I beg I may call him mine, Mr. Bentley, gives me very great concern ; and a train of very melancholy ideas succeeds in my mind, unconnected indeed with your loss, but which still at times casts a shadow over me, which nothing but exertion in business or in acquiring knowledge can remove. This exertion I must recommend to you, as it for a time dispossesses the disagreeable ideas of our loss ; and gradually their impression or effect upon us becomes thus weakened, till the traces are scarcely perceptible, and a scar only is left, which reminds us of the past pain of the united wound.

Mr. Bentley was possessed of such variety of knowledge that his loss is a public calamity, as well as to his friends, though they must feel it the most sensibly. Pray pass a day or two with me at Lichfield, if you can spare the time, at your return. I want much to see you ; and was truly sorry I was from home as you went up ; but I do beg you will always lodge at my house on your road, as I do at yours, whether you meet with me at home or not.

I have searched in vain in Melmoth's translation of Cicero's letters for the famous consolatory letter of Sulpicius to Cicero on the loss of his daughter (as the work has no index), but have found it, the first letter in a small publication called *Letters on the most common as well as important occasions in Life :* Newberry, St. Paul's, 1758. This letter is a masterly piece of oratory indeed, adapted to the man, the time, and the occasion. I think it contains everything which could be said upon the subject, and if you have not seen it, I beg you to send for the book.

For my own part, too sensible of the misfortunes of others for my own happiness, and too pertinacious of the remembrance of my own, I am rather in a situation to demand than to administer consolation. Adieu. God bless you, and believe me, dear Sir, your affectionate friend, E. DARWIN.

The reference in the last paragraph of this letter is to the death of his own son, Charles, about whom we shall hear later. A succession of sorrows made the doctor change his opinion of Sulpicius; for when Edgeworth lost his daughter in 1790, Darwin, in a like situation, was beyond the solace of literature:

Dear Edgeworth,

I much condole with you on your late loss. I know how to feel for your misfortune. . . .

Nil admirari may be a means to escape misery, but not to procure happiness. There is not much to be had in this world—we *expect* too much.

I have had my loss also ! The letter of Sulpicius to Cicero is fine eloquence, but comes not to the heart ; it tugs, but does not draw the arrow. Pains and diseases of the mind are only cured by Time. Reason but skins the wound, which is perpetually liable to fester again. . . .

After Bentley's death Darwin and Wedgwood were greater friends than ever. As far as it was possible for him to do so, Darwin took Bentley's place in Wedgwood's affection; and it is to Josiah that we owe Wright's painting of Erasmus. Their friendship indeed was epoch-making. For the potter's daughter, Susannah, married the doctor's son, Robert, and the result of their union was Charles Darwin.

CHAPTER VII

THE "LUNATICS" [1]

THERE was company at Great Barr House, Mr. Samuel Galton's beautiful country residence in Staffordshire. An enormous log fire was blazing in the dining-room, where, dinner in progress, a number of gentlemen and a few ladies were seated round the table. As one of the courses was being served, the conversation languished, and two or three of the guests became aware of a faint hissing sound. By degrees the sound increased and was accompanied by others of a scraping and tapping nature. When everybody's attention had been drawn to the curious noises, a large black snake darted from under the table and began to range the room.

" Let it alone; it's quite harmless," said one of the company.

But the hostess disliked the idea of a snake at large among her guests. Assured that it was not venomous, and, being by birth a Barclay, anxious to test the practical value of a Quaker's upbringing, she said to her daughter:

" Mary Anne, go and catch that snake."

Putting her trust in God, and thinking hard of the inspiring example set by Mr. Thomas Day in *Sandford and Merton*, Mary Anne (aged about ten) stalked

[1] *See Appendix.*

96

the snake. After a great deal of wriggling on the part of the snake and grabbing on the part of Mary Anne, she managed to round it up, and was rewarded by the praise of the company, one of whom claimed its proprietorship.

"I was riding along the road," he said, "when I observed the animal, as I thought, frozen to death on the side of a bank. I intended to dissect it when I got home; but the warmth of this room has thawed it." Then, turning to Mary Anne, he added: "As a reward for your prowess, you shall keep it."

Meanwhile the butler had gravely noted the proceedings, and at a favourable moment he gave a circumstantial account of them in the servants' hall, concisely summing up the situation with the words: "What can you expect of them lunatics?"

The company of gentlemen thus designated was none other than the famous Lunar Society. In some way unknown to us, Dr. Darwin got to hear of the nickname given the society by Mr. Galton's butler and promptly appropriated it. In a letter to Matthew Boulton from Derby in 1782 he repines: "I am here cut off from the milk of science, which flows in such redundant streams from your learned Lunatics, and which, I can assure you, is a very great regret to me."

The Lunar Society was started by Dr. Darwin. He was its leading light, its dominant personality, its patriarch. It consisted of certain gentlemen, drawn together by a common interest in progress, in science and the arts. They called themselves the Lunar Society because the time of their meeting was near the full moon, so that they might have the benefit of its light in returning home. The meetings took place at one another's houses and lasted from two in the afternoon till about eight in the evening. It was, in many respects, the most remarkable society or group of men in modern history, and the tragedy for us is that it contained no Boswell. By its works, not its words, it is remembered. Its meetings were productive of experiments, inventions, and discoveries that have changed the face of civilization. We shall never know the extent of its influence on the individual achievements of its members. A hint of that influence appears in a letter from Joseph Priestley, which shall be quoted when we come to him.

In actual achievement, in their effect on the history of man, there can of course be no comparison between the Lunar Society and that other great society of the period—the club of which Dr. Johnson was the Darwin. The comparison is anyhow unnecessary because the aims and objects of the two societies were entirely different. It might almost be said that their radical difference lay in the fact that one had certain aims and objects, and the other had not. The society was a meeting of talkers for a purpose; the club was a meeting of talkers for pleasure. And while the former always found pleasure in their purpose, the latter only sometimes found a purpose in their pleasure.

When we come to the individual members of the two groups, we may make as many comparisons as we like. We may, if we wish, compare, in their ultimate benefit to mankind, Watt's separate condenser with

Burke's speeches, Priestley's discovery of oxygen with the portraits of Reynolds, Wedgwood's pots with Garrick's plays, and Darwin's evolution with Johnson's epigrams. But such comparisons are profitless. The point here is that Burke would have been Burke, Reynolds would have been Reynolds, Garrick would have been Garrick, and Johnson would have been Johnson, if the club had never existed; whereas Watt, Priestley, and the rest owed a great deal to Darwin and the Lunar Society.

In the absence of a contemporary Boswell we can only see the figures of Darwin's great society in silhouette. But as no one has so far attempted to portray the group together, let us try to catch a glimpse of them at Barr, their favourite place of meeting. Mr. Galton's house stood on the border of Sutton Coldfield, then a vast wooded chase, seven or eight miles from Birmingham. The spires of Lichfield Cathedral could be seen a dozen miles off from the high ground at the back of the house. The place was therefore within easy reach of Dr. Darwin, and the rest of the "Lunatics" lived in or near Birmingham.

Samuel Galton was born in 1753. At the age of fifteen he went to the Warrington Academy, where Dr. Priestley taught. He then entered his father's business in Birmingham. His one brother and six sisters died young, so he inherited the whole of his father's property. The Galtons were Quakers and got themselves into hot water with their co-religionists "for fabricating and selling instruments of war." Samuel disregarded the warnings he had received and at last was formally disowned by the Society of Friends. Whereupon he proved that he was not a friend of Dr. Darwin's for nothing by writing a tract, in which he pointed out that for seventy years his grandfather, his uncle, and his father had been engaged in that trade without any complaints from the Society and that he had merely inherited the business. Further, he informed them that to be consistent no member of the Society ought to pay taxes to a Government which prepared for war, or preserved the peace in times of riot. " Men," said he, " are not responsible for the abuse of what they manufacture." He flatly declined to give any pledge to the Society that he would cease fabricating and selling instruments of war and declared that if ever he decided to abandon the business it should be because he wanted to do so, not because he was told to do so. In short, he was a real Quaker.

Privately, Galton entirely disregarded the disownment, went on attending the meetings until his death nearly forty years later, and continued his annual donations—which were too generous for the Society to refuse.

Galton was keen on optics, made many colour-mixing experiments, and hit on the idea of three primary colours before the supposed originator. He had a mania for mechanical improvements, and, like the rest of the " Lunatics," he loved making experiments.

Every inch a host, he would sit at the head of the table, listening to as much of the conversation as he could catch, with his mind on a dozen subjects at once. He had a strong face, a large nose, clearly cut features, and quick, eager eyes. Insatiably curious about everything, he would change the topic of conversation continually, jumping from chemistry to the rights of man, from botany to the tyranny of parents. He watched the effects of his remarks on his friends, and propounded problems for the mere pleasure of hearing their solutions. His attitude to nearly every question could be summed up in the phrase: Here is a subject on which we may sharpen our wits. Once the question of miracles in the Bible was introduced. "It is contrary to universal experience that miracles should take place," said he. He paused for a moment, playing with his eyeglass, then added: "but it is according to all experience that men should lie." That was the way to start an interesting train of conjectures, and it always came off. . . .

Seated near him was a very different type of man; one who talked for the sake of reaching a definite conclusion, who preferred an ounce of fact to a ton of theory. This was James Keir, Darwin's oldest friend, who, more than any one except the doctor, had been responsible for the formation of the Lunar Society. A solid man was Keir, on whom people made a habit of leaning when they were in difficulties. He was, perhaps, the only member of the orthodox Church in the society.

The youngest of eighteen children, James Keir was born in Edinburgh in 1735, and educated at the high school and university there. He met Erasmus Darwin at the university and they instantly became fast friends. He told Darwin that he was tired of Scotland, and especially of Edinburgh, and wanted above all things to visit foreign countries. He therefore joined the army in order to see the world; but the nations of Europe could not oblige him with a war on the spur of the moment, so his Wanderlust was confined to the West Indies and Ireland. While in the West Indies he caught yellow fever. Through the window of the hospital ship in which he lay he could see the sharks tearing to pieces the bodies of his companions who had died of the same disease. One day the army surgeon came into his cabin, and, finding him both speechless and motionless, decided his number was up and issued the necessary instructions. Keir, however, revived a little, and when someone came to pitch him overboard he made a sign that he wished to write. A pencil was brought and he wrote a request for a certain quantity of antimony. The use of antimony as a medicine was then unknown, but as he was regarded as a hopeless case, the request was granted. He recovered.

While in the army, he used to get up at four in the morning, study the classics, translate Polybius, and compile a treatise on the art of war. Much to his chagrin, his brother officers displayed no sympathy with his classical studies, and after eleven years he left the army and turned his attention to chemistry. When he was stationed in Ireland he wrote letters to Darwin, in one of which he said: "If I come now, my principal, or rather sole inducement, will be a visit that I have long been desirous to make to you." One is not surprised therefore that he settled in the Darwin country and was soon on intimate terms with the Darwin circle. His translation of Macquer's *Dictionary of*

Chemistry was hailed with delight by the "Lunatics," to many of whom it proved invaluable. His personal popularity among them may be gauged by a paragraph in a letter he received from Boulton, dated 1 March, 1777:

Pray, where were you the last full moon? I hope you were not influenced by any influenza to stay at home. I saw Darwin yesterday at Lichfield. He desires to know if you will come to Soho on Sunday, the 3rd March, in which case he will not fail to meet you, although he says he has inoculated some children which will probably be ill about that time. Yet if you will come he will be at Soho by eleven o'clock, when I propose to make several motions to the members. Pray God bless your fireside, and preserve it from smoking and falling chimneys, and every other terrestrial evil. Yours sincerely and affectionately, MATTHEW BOULTON.

Keir was closely in touch with Watt and Priestley while they were experimenting with gas, water, acids, air, etc., and they were constantly writing to him for the result of his own researches. He shrank from celebrity, and when some of his discoveries in chemistry were attributed to others, he refused to claim them, saying to such friends as pressed him to do so: " Knowledge is important, but whether the discovery is made by one man or another is not deserving of consideration."

At the Lunar meetings he seems to have been a sort of unofficial chairman. Members would apply to him for a decision in a debate, because they trusted his judgment and recognized his impartiality and love of truth. His was a tranquil nature. When he heard that his house was burnt down owing to the carelessness of his clerks, who, when they went to bed, used to rake the fire out on to the hearthstone, his sole remark was: " The safest place for a fire is—*the grate*."

He was a wit, too, a man of the world, who could at need placate or animate a meeting. Above all, he was steady and absolutely reliable. When Day died, his wife asked Keir to write his Life. Keir applied to Edgeworth for material. Edgeworth, fortunately for us, saw the funny side of Day and sent a batch of amusing anecdotes to Keir. A correspondence ensued. Keir was jealous for the reputation of his friend, refused to let him be laughed at, and returned the anecdotes. A final letter from Edgeworth explains why Keir's biography of Day is so dull:

We differ so materially in our ideas of private biography —you believing that nothing but what concerns the public should be published, I thinking that to entertain mankind is no inefficacious method of instructing them. When Mason was reproached by somebody for publishing the private letters of Gray, he answered, " Would you always have my friends appear in full dress ? " I might quote Plutarch as well as Mason in support of my opinion ; but I am sure you must perceive, my dear sir, that I am not willing to enter into any literary competition with you, well knowing my inferiority. R. L. E.

But Mrs. Day believed Keir to be thoroughly dependable; she had heard her husband say so, and her husband was never wrong. In this case, assuredly, he was not.

Keir always kept his head, even when all the scientists round him were losing theirs in the excitement of new

discoveries. Darwin sometimes made the most sweep-
ing assertions in the cause of science, which, in any
other case, he would have been the first to poke fun at.
Keir pulled him up sharply once:

" You are such an infidel in religion, my dear doctor,
that you cannot believe in transubstantiation; yet you
can believe that apples and pears, hay and oats, bread
and wine, sugar, oil and vinegar, are nothing but water
and charcoal, and that it is a great improvement in
language to call all these things by one word—oxide
hydro-carbonneux."

On another occasion, when Darwin had in his usual
manner been praising the French Revolution and Bonaparte, and criticizing Keir's *Reflections on the Invasion
of Great Britain by the French Armies*, the author of
that pamphlet genially observed:

" I suppose, like Archimedes when Syracuse was
taken and soldiers rushed into his house, you will tell
the French, *when* they come to Derby, not to disturb
your meditations; and that you are just on the point
of catching the *matter* of electricity by the tail, and the
matter of heat by its whiskers."

Such, then, was James Keir. By nature gentle, but
not easily led, his character could be seen in his face,
with its wide, ample nose, kindly eyes, plump cheeks,
full chin, and general expression of placid good-nature.
He was one of the few " Lunatics" who survived well
into the nineteenth century, and the verdict of the new
generation upon him was delivered by Sir Humphry
Davy. When quite a young man Davy called upon
Keir one day, noted his kindliness of heart and

independence of mind, and was extremely sorry to leave him, for he was "both an amiable and a great man."

At the age of eighty-two he wrote a philosophical poem on the *Periods of Human Life*, in which this verse occurs:

> Friends of my youth ! Where are ye ? Fled from hence ;
> And I a stranger in my native plain !
> A breathing monument of man remain !
> Joy, hope, and passion, cease to rouse my sense.

But at the age of eighty-five, on his death-bed, he was not too old to learn; for he asked his servant to read aloud the New Testament " to instruct him."

Perhaps the most vocal guest at Mr. Galton's house was Richard Lovell Edgeworth. A handsome man, with well-proportioned features, and "aristocrat" written all over him. Very full of himself, rather conceited, extremely courteous—almost histrionically so— and eminently clubbable. Might easily have been the Boswell of his circle. He was introduced by Keir to another social group of that period, which met at Slaughter's Coffee House in London, and included Sir Joseph Banks, Captain Cook, and other famous folk. The qualification for membership was peculiar. " We practised," says Edgeworth, " every means in our power, except personal insult, to try the temper and understanding of each candidate for admission. Every prejudice, which his profession or situation in life might have led him to cherish, was attacked, exposed to argument and ridiculed. The argument was always ingenious, and the ridicule sometimes coarse." Thus only a very conceited or a very unassuming person could pass the test.

Edgeworth was an entertaining fellow, and popular within limits; but he did not wear so well as Watt or Keir. The new generation, in the person of Lord Byron, rather wanted to kick him. Edgeworth came in late to breakfast at Sir Humphry Davy's and boasted that he had given Dr. Parr a dressing-down the night before. The poet, who was present, notes in his Journal: " . . . Old Edgeworth a bore—the worst of all bores—a boisterous bore."

Wedgwood, though not a regular "Lunatic," sometimes graced the board with his cheerful, honest face; and Day, who came frequently before his marriage, would sit awkwardly at table, either wrapped in gloomy silence, with cloudy countenance, or monologising at length, in solemn periods, on the wickedness of man and the shallowness of woman.

Then we notice Dr. Small, whom all the "Lunatics" loved; and Dr. Stoke, who was so absent-minded that he put a snake in his pocket and forgot all about it; and Dr. Johnson (a clergyman, not Samuel), who won Priestley's heart by talking of the Trinity like a sensible human being; and Dr. Withering, who knew all about flowers and medicine, bred dogs and cattle, and prolonged his frail existence by living his last years in his library with a uniform temperature of 65 degrees Fahrenheit, during which it was said "The Flower of Physic is indeed Withering"; and John Whitehurst, the horologer, who ventilated St. Thomas's Hospital, made a clock for the town hall at Derby, wrote an *Enquiry into the Original State and Formation of the Earth*, and pursued his researches beneath the earth's surface with such ardour that his health was impaired by the constant exposure; and others whose names we cannot even catch. . . .

But there were three men who seldom missed a Lunar meeting at Mr. Galton's or anywhere else, and whose names are as familiar to us as to their friends.

First, we note that splendid-looking fellow, with the lofty carriage, grand manner and massive dignity of a nobleman of the *ancien régime*. Indeed, with his superb forehead, widely set eyes, open, distinguished countenance, and king-like calm, he might easily be mistaken for Louis XIV himself. We have already been introduced to him. His name: Matthew Boulton.

The first great metal manufacturer of England, he had started life in a small way, but reached by quick stages an extraordinary pre-eminence. His works at Soho, just outside Birmingham, became one of the wonders of the empire. Beginning with vases, candelabra, snuff-boxes, buckles, silver and plated goods, he was soon perfecting the crafts of bronzing, enamelling, and steel-inlaying. At times he came into open competition with Wedgwood, though their friendship remained unimpaired. "It doubles my courage," wrote Wedgwood to Bentley, "to have the first manufacturer in England to incounter with. The match likes me well—I like the man—I like his spirit —he will not be a mere drivelling copyist like the antagonists I have hitherto made, but will venture to step out of the lines upon occasion, and afford us some diversion in the combat."

Matthew had an enormous opinion of himself and all that he called his. Soho, where he lived and had his works, was Paradise. He would chant pæans to the glory of Soho. He had turned it from a rabbit-warren into a garden-city. No wonder his own work-men called him the "Prince of Soho." Of course he lived up to the part; he dressed like a prince, talked like a prince, walked like a prince, and looked like a prince. "Mr. Boulton has not yet sent any of his things to St. James's," Wedgwood confides to his partner; " he soars higher, and is scheming to be sent for by his Majesty."

His ambitious designs led him into the realm of exaggeration. Everything he did had to be a little more magnificent than it actually was; so he embroidered on facts with all the fancy of a poet. Wedgwood once caught him out in a frightful lie, but inwardly said, " Well done, Boulton!" He was the lord of his little world, and wore an air of command wherever he went, taking the lead in conversation and having his own way in everything.

With the advent of Watt, Boulton rose to still giddier heights. The whole working force of Soho was now concentrated upon the construction and improvement of the steam-engine. His rivalry with Wedgwood was at an end, and the potter wrote to Bentley: " Certain steam-engines have lifted a good friend of ours above his watch-chain and sleeve-button business."

But Boulton's really great qualities now came into play. He believed in Watt and backed him almost to the point of bankruptcy. Within four years he had to find £6000 for the costs of legal actions to prevent infringements of their patents. He borrowed money right and left (£5000 from Wedgwood, among others) and worked like a slave to achieve the grand object of his life. His generosity and imagination were balanced by insight, and he won the battle after many years of desperate struggle.

Among other things, he supplied the machinery for the new mint on Tower Hill and undertook the production of the new copper coinage for Great Britain. His energies in this direction won a notable tribute from Darwin:

"If a civic crown was given in Rome for preserving the life of one citizen," said the doctor, "Mr. Boulton should be covered with garlands of oak!"

The compliment may sound a trifle obscure until it is explained that Boulton had invented a new process of coining money which utterly defeated the counterfeiters, who, prior to his invention, were being executed by the dozen for false coining!

When it was Boulton's turn to hold a meeting of the Lunar Society at his house, he managed things on a lavish scale. Then, indeed, he would be seen in all his pride, power, and magnificence, dispensing a regal hospitality in his own palace, among his own people, as to the manner born. It must have been a blow to him when he received such a letter as this from Dr. Darwin, dated 5 April, 1778:

Dear Boulton,

I am sorry the infernal divinities who visit mankind with diseases, and are therefore at perpetual war with doctors, should have prevented my seeing all your great men at Soho to-day. Lord! what inventions, what wit, what rhetoric, metaphysical, mechanical, and pyrotechnical, will be on the wing, bandied like a shuttlecock from one to another of your troop of philosophers! while poor I, I by myself, I, imprisoned in a postchaise, am joggled, and jostled, and bumped and bruised along the King's high-road, to make war upon a stomach-ache or a fever!

Though he could not easily brook opposition, Mr. Boulton was strangely attentive to the opinions of one man—a man who sat with his head on his hands, his shoulders rounded, his chest fallen in, whose limbs were lank and unmuscular, whose complexion was sallow, who drooped, and who bore on his face the unmistakable signs of constant ill-health and constitutional melancholia. This was James Watt, to whom Mr. Boulton frequently referred and usually deferred. Nearly every characteristic of the manufacturer was absent in the inventor, and vice versa. Self-assurance and enthusiasm were the marked qualities of the first; humility and pessimism were those of the second.

In a company where James Watt was unknown, he would have passed unnoticed. He would meditate for hours, hardly shifting his position. His face would seldom light up with pleasure; at the most a wrinkle would deepen from his nose to the corner of his mouth, which denoted that he was less unhappy than usual. His steady gaze was a little disconcerting to the stranger who thought that he was the object of Watt's calm contemplation, and who failed to realize that the quiet Scot was looking *through* him and was only partially aware of his existence.

James Watt was born in 1736. As a child he was delicate, and all through life he was subject to severe headaches, which at times made existence almost insupportable. He suffered so greatly from mental fatigue that he usually required ten hours' sleep out of every twenty-four. But he was a determined and persistent man, who merely stood in need of constant encouragement. His gentle, modest, unassuming manners, his slow and unimpassioned speech, deep and low in tone, and the music of his broad Scottish accent, made friends for him wherever he went. He was loved by all the "Lunatics," though his lack of geniality prevented him from being what is commonly called popular.

He first entered the charmed circle in 1767, when he passed through Birmingham on his way home from London, where he had been spending several months on business connected with the Forth and Clyde canal. He called on Darwin at Lichfield and was so enchanted by his host that, there and then, he confided his great secret to the doctor. Shortly after he left for Scotland, in August 1767, Darwin wrote:

Now, my dear new friend, I first hope you are well and less hypochondriacal, and that Mrs. Watt and your child are well. The plan of your steam improvements I have religiously kept secret, but begin myself to see some difficulties in your execution which did not strike me when you were here. I have got another and another new hobby-horse since I saw you. I wish the Lord would send you to pass a week with me—a week, a month, a year! You promised to send me an instrument to draw landscapes with. If you ever move your place of residence for any long time from Glasgow, pray acquaint me. Adieu. Your friend, E. DARWIN.

A year later Watt spent a fortnight with Boulton at Birmingham and again enjoyed the society of Darwin. Then he joined hands with Boulton, and the great era of steam had begun.

Watt remained all his life a scientific investigator. When not busy with his engine he would turn his attention to such widely dissimilar things as the composition of water, which he discovered, and a letter-copying machine, which he invented. But he had no use whatever for anything outside science. Music he called "the source of idleness" and he would probably have allowed his face a wrinkle if he could have heard his countryman, Carlyle's, contemptuous definition of it: "Twiddle-de-deeing on melodious catgut." He hated business and finance, and once lost his temper when pressed to take part in an agitation against taxes, urging as an excuse for his abstention: "We seem to be fast approaching first to the maximum of taxes, and I hope still faster to the maximum of national patience; when matters are at the worst they must mend."

Other countries were quick to recognize his genius and he was invited to Russia. Darwin heard of it and lost no time in raising his voice against it:

Lord, how frightened I was when I heard a Russian bear had laid hold of you with his great paw, and was dragging you to Russia! Pray don't go if you can help it. Russia is like the den of Cacus : you see the footsteps of many beasts going thither, but of few returning. I hope your fire-engines will keep you here.

But Darwin need not have worried. Watt was far too fond of his workshop in Soho, and the financial protection of Boulton, to leave either for "a business proposition" in Russia.

Considering that he was the founder and most versatile member of the Lunar Society, Darwin's frequent absences from its meetings must have vexed his philosophic brethren. Watt wrote to him on 3 January, 1781, from Birmingham:

I beg that you would impress on your memory the idea that you promised to dine with sundry men of learning at my house on Monday next, and that you will realize that idea. For your encouragement, there is a new book to cut up; and it is to be determined whether or not heat is a compound of phlogiston and empyreal air, and whether a mirror can reflect the heat of the fire. I give you a friendly warning that you may be found wanting, whichever opinion you adopt in the latter question; therefore be cautious. If you are meek and humble, perhaps you may be told what light is made of, and the theory proved both by synthesis and analysis.

To which Darwin replied on 6 January from Beau-Desert:

You know there is a perpetual war carried on between the devil and all holy men. Sometimes one prevails in an odd skirmish or so, and sometimes the other. Now, you must know this said devil has played me a slippery trick, and, I fear, prevented me from coming to join the holy men at your house, by sending the measles with peripneumony amongst

nine beautiful children of Lord Paget's. For I must suppose
it is a work of the devil! Surely the Lord could never think
of amusing himself by setting nine little animals to cough
their hearts up? Pray ask your learned society if this partial
evil contributes to any public good—if this pain is necessary
to establish the subordination of different links in the chain
of animation? If one was to be weaker and less perfect than
another, must he therefore have pain as a part of his portion?
Pray inquire of your philosophers, and rescue me from
Manichæism.

As to material philosophy, I can tell you some secrets in
return for yours; viz. that atmospheric air is composed of
light, and the earth of water (and aqueous earth). That
water is composed of aqueous gas, which is displaced from its
earth by oil of vitriol.

Pray make my best devoirs to all the philosophers, and pray
tell Dr. Priestley that I wish he would try whether a plant
insulated in ☿ will spoil air.

Darwin published the second part of his poem *The
Botanic Garden* before the first. It was called *The
Loves of the Plants* and was an immediate success.
So he decided to follow it up as quickly as possible
with the first part, *The Economy of Vegetation*, and
wrote to Watt:

As *The Loves of the Plants pays* me well, and as I
write for pay, not for fame, I intend to publish *The
Economy of Vegetation* in the spring. Now in this work
I shall in a note mention something about steam-engines,
which may occupy 2 or 3 pages. The historical part . . .
I think to abstract from Harris's Lexicon and Chambers's
Dictionary. But what must I add about Messrs. Watt and
Boulton? This is the question. Now, if you will at a
leisure hour tell me what the world may know about your
improvements of the steam-engine, or anything about your

experiments, or calculated facts about the power of your engines, or any other *ingenious stuff* for a note, I shall with pleasure insert it, *either with or without your name,* as you please.

If you do not take this trouble, I must make worse work of it myself, and celebrate your engines as well as I can. I wish the whole not to exceed 2 or 3 quarto pages, and to consist of such facts, or things, as may be rather *agreeable*; I mean *gentlemanlike* facts, not abstruse calculations only fit for philosophers.

I hope you use the warm bath, and enjoy better health, and ride some furious hobby-horse. I am sorry I cannot see you oftener; it is a great loss to my understanding, and to my happiness. The Lord keep you! Adieu! From yours affectionately, E. DARWIN.

Note his reference to a hobby-horse once more. He clearly perceived that Watt had no interests outside his experiments and that this was a danger to his health. Watt replied:

I know not how steam-engines come among the plants; I cannot find them in the *Systema Naturæ,* by which I should conclude that they are neither plants, animals, nor fossils, otherwise they could not have escaped the notice of Linnæus. However, if they belong to *your* system, no matter about the Swede; and your kind attention to us will certain make me furnish you with all the necessary materials for poetic readers, with a wish that something else in the author way would pay you better than poetry, though no man possesses a more amiable Muse, and you are a happy man that still find yourself equal to the embraces of such a frolicsome damsel! . . .

I join in your wish that we could meet oftener; I should be the greatest gainer of the two. . . . Yours affectionately, JAMES WATT.

The friendship of these two men deepened with the

years, and Watt once told a friend that Darwin "was almost my most ancient acquaintance and friend in England, I having been intimate with him for thirty-four years and on many occasions much indebted to his good offices." His final tribute to Darwin does credit to them both: "For my part," said the great engineer, "it will be my pride, while I live, that I have enjoyed the friendship of such a man. . . ."

Darwin drew him out, made him take an interest in things that had no relation to science. Up to middle age his knowledge, though great in matters of utility, was confined to utilitarian matters. Thus, he could tell an artist that rats' whiskers made good painting-brushes, and could instruct people how to warm a house, cure a smoking chimney, obtain fast colours, or improve a jews' harp. Once, when in Paris, he visited the Tuileries. There he joined several people who were listening to the complaints of a maid concerning some English stoves which had just been received and which she was unable to clean. At last she appealed for advice to an English gentleman who was standing by, whose name was Charles James Fox. "I fear," he replied, "that I cannot help you, but here is a fellow-countryman of mine who will tell you all about it"—and he pushed forward Mr. Watt, who at once gave the maid all the information she required.

But under Darwin he broadened out; and, living well into the next century, left an impression of extra-ordinary versatility on the mind of Sir Walter Scott, who, looking back in later years, wrote the great engineer's best epitaph:

" It was only once my fortune to meet him. . . . There were assembled about half a score of our Northern Lights. . . . Amidst this company stood Mr. Watt, the man whose genius discovered the means of multiplying our national resources to a degree perhaps even beyond his own stupendous powers of calculation and combination; bringing the treasures of the abyss to the summit of the earth—giving the feeble arm of man the momentum of an Afrite—commanding manufactures to arise, as the rod of the prophet produced water in the desert, affording the means of dispensing with that time and tide which wait for no man, and of sailing without that wind which defied the commands and threats of Xerxes himself. This potent commander of the elements—this abridger of time and space—this magician, whose cloudy machinery has produced a change on the world, the effects of which, extraordinary as they are, are perhaps only now beginning to be felt —was not only the most profound man of science, the most successful combiner of powers and calculator of numbers, as adapted to practical purposes—was not only one of the most generally well-informed—but one of the best and kindest human beings.

" There he stood, surrounded by the little band I have mentioned of Northern *literati*, men not less tenacious, generally speaking, of their own fame and their own opinions, than the national regiments are supposed to be jealous of the high character which they have won upon service. Methinks I yet see and hear what I shall never see or hear again. In his eighty-fifth year, the alert, kind, benevolent old man, had his attention alive to everyone's question, his information at everyone's command.

" His talents and fancy overflowed on every subject. One gentleman was a deep philologist—he talked with him on the origin of the alphabet as if he had been coeval with Cadmus; another a celebrated critic—you would have said the old man had studied political economy and *belles-lettres* all his life; of science it is unnecessary to speak, it was his own distinguished walk. And yet . . . when he spoke with your countryman . . . you would have sworn he had been coeval with Claver'se and Burley, with the persecutors and persecuted, and could number every shot the dragoons had fired at the fugitive Covenanters. In fact, we discovered that no novel of the least celebrity escaped his perusal, and that the gifted man of science was as much addicted to the productions of your native country . . . as shameless and obstinate a peruser of novels, as if he had been a very milliner's apprentice of eighteen." . . .

In strong contrast with the radiant benignity of Boulton and the melancholy solemnity of Watt, was the mercurial curiosity of Priestley. While Boulton beamed and Watt frowned, Priestley stammered with excitement. He was so thrilled by his own thoughts that he would forget time, forget to dine, forget everything except the idea of the moment. He would sit up till two, three, four in the morning, discussing with intense eagerness the Trinity or electricity, never for a moment forgetting the proper aim of all discussion— a desire to reach the truth, not a desire to beat an antagonist—and never, therefore, losing his temper.

Though his expressions in controversy were frequently a little pointed, his desire was always to make his opponent as candid as himself, for truth, in his view, could not be reached by way of mere politeness. He continually dwelt on the blessings of free inquiry, and even went so far as to say that, so long as everyone was occupied in the search after truth, it mattered little if all arrived at different conclusions. It is, however, just possible he did not altogether approve Darwin's conclusion about his co-religionists. "Unitarianism," said the doctor, "is a feather-bed to catch a falling Christian."

As he often stammered in his speech, so did he often break into a trot when he was out for a walk. A country ramble with him was just as fruitful of ideas as an evening by the fireside. He would walk quickly, or half run, with head bent forward, observing everything, from a shadow cast by the clouds to a half-hidden flower in the cleft of a rock—taking delight in everything, talking of everything. A charming companion at all times, though possibly a little trying over the early morning toast and marmalade. He had a pointed nose, a slightly receding chin, eyes that radiated joy, and a seraphic smile. Looked at in profile, one side of his face was entirely different from the other. In social converse his whole countenance was alive and animated to such a degree that one observer called his expression "celestial."

Born in 1733, Joseph Priestley was already showing a peculiar interest in oxygen at the age of eleven; for he put spiders in bottles to see how long they could live without fresh air. Before he was twenty he knew the Hebrew Bible and while still in his 'teens was distressed that he could not feel a proper repentance for the Sin of Adam. He learned to play the flute, and as he had no ear for music, this gave him great pleasure. He was ordained as a dissenting minister in 1762. The Sheffield dissenters rejected him because he was "too gay and airy," but he got a job at Leeds. An old lady in his congregation there thought she was possessed of a devil, and, believing that he could perform miracles, begged him to cure her. He at once assented, and exorcised the devil with the aid of an electric shock.

He advocated an increasing number of religious sects, toleration for papists, and even concurred in the formation of the Unitarian Society, which he joined. By this time, however, he had written innumerable pamphlets on the Trinity, and had almost succeeded in explaining it away to his own satisfaction.

His essential simplicity of character was displayed on an occasion when, in moving from Leeds to Calne (to become librarian to Lord Shelburne), he offered to help his wife to pack their things. She told him that when she had finished the packing, he could fasten and cord the boxes. He did so. Upon arrival at their new home, she undid the boxes, and discovered to her dismay that under the cover of each box her husband had packed specimens of minerals and a number of chemical mixtures. She pointed to the clothes, which were in an appalling state, but he hurriedly begged her not to distress herself, as the minerals and mixtures had survived the journey in admirable condition!

As this may suggest he was more of a scientist than a human being, the following story will prove the contrary. He was occupied on his first and most important investigation into the composition of air, when he was suddenly called away from home. He charged his wife, and the housemaid, not on any account to disturb his study, where he was leaving the inverted glasses which contained the gases immersed in water. The housemaid, interpreting the command that nothing should be disturbed into one that everything should be put in order, carefully removed, cleaned, and wiped the glasses, and placed them neatly on the shelf. Mrs. Priestley was horrified when she discovered what had been done, and wondered how on earth to break the news to her husband. When he returned, she told him to prepare for a shock. He prepared. But when she had delivered it, he showed intense relief, said that he was afraid she was going to say one of the children was seriously ill, that it would only cost him a few weeks' labour, and that if someone else should make the discovery first, it didn't matter in the least, as it would be equally useful to the world. . . .

Though Priestley could charm away the bitterest prejudices in personal intercourse, he was powerless against the hatred his doctrines provoked. In the year 1791 a terrible thing happened to our philosophers in Birmingham. It was the cause of Priestley's ultimate removal to America, where he died.

Perhaps it is hardly necessary to say that the French Revolution had been hailed by the "Lunatics" as the dawn of a new and more enlightened age. "I have seen," said a lady who lived through that period, " the reception of the news of the victory of Waterloo, and of the carrying of the Reform Bill, but I never saw joy comparable in its vivid intensity and universality to that occasioned by the early promise of the French Revolution." Even as late as 1792, Darwin said: " In spite of all their disasters, the cause of freedom will triumph, and France become, ere long, an example prosperous, as great, to the surrounding nations." Equally, the "Lunatics" had been on the side of America in the War of Independence, and both Darwin and Priestley were friends and admirers of Benjamin Franklin.

Priestley had written a vigorous reply to Burke's fatuous *Reflections* on the French Revolution, and it may be said that the behaviour of the mob at Birmingham in July 1791, was largely the result of the hostility Priestley had aroused among the Churchmen and Conservatives throughout the country by his religious and political opinions. What happened can be told quickly.

The following advertisement appeared in *Aris's Birmingham Gazette*:

Hotel, Birmingham, July 7, 1791.

Commemoration of the French Revolution.

A number of gentlemen intend dining together on the 14th inst., to commemorate the auspicious day which witnessed the emancipation of 26 millions of people from the yoke of despotism and restored the blessings of equal Government to a truly great and enlightened nation ; with whom it is our interest as a commercial people, and our duty as friends to the general rights of mankind, to promote a free intercourse as subservient to a permanent friendship.

Any friend to Freedom disposed to join the intended temperate festivity is desired to leave his name at the bar of the hotel, where tickets may be had at 5s. each, including a bottle of wine ; but no person will be admitted without one.

Dinner will be on the table at 3 o'clock precisely.

This advertisement was followed by a circular, which was printed and distributed by the enemies of the commemorators, in order to provoke public feeling against them.

On Thursday, 14 July, 1791, eighty-one gentlemen arrived at the hotel and were served with dinner. James Keir was in the chair. A crowd of people had collected round the hotel previous to the dinner and each member of the party had been greeted with hissing. Priestley was not present. Several toasts were drunk, including one to "The Prince of Wales: may he have the wisdom to prefer the glory of being the chief of an entire and free people to that of being the splendid fountain of corruption." Altogether there were nineteen toasts, and it may be doubted whether the wine ration included in the five-shilling bill of fare was sufficient to cover the lot. In a letter to the *Birmingham and Staffordshire Chronicle* a week or two later, James Keir scouted the notion that there had been any disloyal or seditious toasts, and mentioned that the first toast was "The King and Constitution" and one of the last was "Peace and Goodwill to all Mankind," which, said he, "cannot easily be interpreted to excite people to tumult." All the toasts had a humanitarian tinge—Poland, France, America, the Rights of Man, Hampden, Sidney, and cognate themes. Several songs were sung, and between five and six the gentlemen peacefully dispersed to their various homes. But the crowd remained and gradually increased. By eight o'clock the hotel was surrounded by a mob, which opened the campaign by smashing all the windows. The sound of breaking glass inspired them to further feats of heroism. Shouting "No philosophers! Church and King for ever!" the rioters proceeded to the New Meeting House, divided up the movables and set it alight. They repeated the performance at the Old Meeting House.

By this time the philosophers had been apprised of the operations in the city. Dr. Withering, who was not at the dinner, packed his books and botanic specimens into several wagons, covered them with hay, and made for the open country.[1] Dr. Priestley was enjoying a cheerful evening with his family when he heard that the rioters were making for his house. They had clamoured for him at the hotel ("We want Priestley!") and as the war was being waged on behalf of the Established Church it was only natural that the leading Dissenter should be asked to explain his precise theological position. Dr. Priestley, however, had been warned that explanations would, under the circumstances, probably be misconstrued, and did not wait to make them. He bolted with his family as the crowd of enthusiastic Churchmen surged up the road.

---

[1] Boulton and Watt armed their employees at the Soho works, barricaded the doors, and prepared to make a stand for philosophy; but they were unmolested.

The furniture of the dissenting minister's house was dragged out and rendered unto Demos, after which the house was burnt to the ground. With the house went all Priestley's laboriously-collected philosophical instruments, his library, and his manuscripts, the result of many years' work and study. In an open letter to his "late townsmen and neighbours," published some weeks after the event, he deplored the loss of his manuscripts, "which I shall never be able to recompose," and asked: "Can you think such conduct as yours any recommendation of your religious principles in preference to ours?" He also asserted that all this had "been done to one who never did or imagined you any harm." But personal sentiment has never been the strong point of Christian soldiers, marching as to war.

After the destruction of Priestley's house the rioters had had enough entertainment for one evening. The following morning saw them at Bordesley Hall, vociferating "Church and King!" and spreading terror in every direction. At Bordesley Hall they were made free of the cellar, in the hope that hospitality would turn their thoughts from more heavenly exercises. For a time it did. While they lay about in drunken stupor their behaviour left nothing to be desired. But the moment the effects of the drink wore off, the architectural beauty of the mansion got on their nerves, and they couldn't resist the temptation to commit arson. Bordesley Hall disappeared in flames.

Now the curious thing is that the authorities omitted to read the Riot Act during the early stages of these transactions. A year later, when a raid on the brothels of Birmingham was contemplated, the Riot Act was read without delay, and the brothels were saved. But it was never satisfactorily explained why brothels were considered more salutary to the communal life of Birmingham than chapels and scientific laboratories. True, the magistrates collected together a number of special constables, who rushed about with sticks and tried to break up the gangs of rioters; but they were quite useless, and only caused a certain amount of skull-fracturing.

A large number of private residences were looted and then illuminated—though none of their owners, with a single exception, had been present at the commemorative dinner—and the rioters, taking advantage of the general consternation, visited every part of the town and relieved the inhabitants of their ready money. Things were going strong right up to Sunday evening, 17 July, when the arrival of regular troops caused an instant reaction to law and order and confined the attention of the looters to the surrounding country. Up to Tuesday, the 19th, bodies of banditti (as they were called by non-Churchmen) were carrying on the good work at King's Norton, Bromsgrove, and Halesowen; but the moment they heard that cavalry was beginning to scour the country, they assumed the demeanour of benevolently-disposed unemployed workmen and got back to their Birmingham homes as fast as they could go without arousing suspicion.

Thus did the lovers of Church, King, and Constitution prove their abhorrence of the French Revolution and all its works. Dr. Darwin regarded their behaviour

in a different light. He said that the Birmingham riots
"were a disgrace to mankind, for active ignorance
delights in repressing the sciences it does not understand." But then Dr. Darwin was a philosopher, and
therefore partial.

Priestley's friends thought it would be dangerous for
him to return to Birmingham for a little while, so he
went to London, where he sat down and wrote an
Address to the Inhabitants of Birmingham. He also wrote an
Appeal, which reviewed the troubles at some length in a
tone of no little asperity. His friends, Keir, Wedgwood,
Galton, Withering, and others, did their best to make
him soften many of the passages. He cut out a certain
amount, but could not bring himself to fall in with
their views on all points. They, of course, wanted
him back among them. He, though equally anxious to
return, would not sacrifice truth to convenience.

Samuel Galton showed his sterling qualities in a
letter he wrote to Priestley six weeks after the riots:

If you incline to come to Birmingham . . . pray inform
me the hour you expect to arrive and where, for I will meet
you at the coach and accompany you in your perambulations
about the town, happy in an occasion to avow the most
explicit attachment to a Person, whose friendship does me
the greatest honour. . . . It shall never be said that Dr.
Priestley was not received with open arms by one on whom
he has conferred such obligations. The idea of fear Mrs.
Galton and myself equally despise, nor do we really think
there is any danger, but if the alternative were that we should
lose our house or our esteem for ourselves, we would not
pause for a moment.

But Priestley never returned to Birmingham. In his

Memoirs he declared: "I consider my settlement at Birmingham as the happiest event of my life," and he enumerated his fellow-members of the Lunar Society who had made it so. To Keir he wrote: "I beg my compliments to the members of the Lunar Society, and as long as I live, I shall, with much satisfaction, think of our many happy meetings." In a letter to Watt he referred to ". . . the pleasing intercourse I have had with you, and all my friends of the Lunar Society. Such another I can never expect to see. Indeed London cannot furnish it. I shall always think of you at the usual time of your meeting."

And in 1793 Priestley dedicated his *Experiments on the Generation of Air from Water* to the members of the Lunar Society, in words with which we too must bid them farewell:

My Valued Friends,

There are few things I more regret, in consequence of my removal from Birmingham, than the loss of your society. It both encouraged and enlightened me ; so that what I did there of a philosophical kind, ought in justice to be attributed almost as much to you as to myself. From our cheerful meetings I never absented myself voluntarily, and from my pleasing recollection they will never be absent. Should the cause of our separation make it necessary or expedient for me to remove to a still greater distance from you, I shall only think the more, and with the more regret, of our past interviews.

It is now more than two years that I have been deprived of your society, and that I have been under the disagreeable necessity of intermitting my philosophical pursuits. With the assistance of my friends I have now resumed them, and it is with particular satisfaction that I dedicate the first fruits of my labours to you.

You are no strangers to the ostensible cause of those disgraceful riots which drove me from your neighbourhood, and you know my perfect innocence with respect to them. Had I really been what the populace, who demolished my library and apparatus, my house and everything belonging to me, were taught to believe, viz. : a fomenter of sedition, and an enemy to the peace and constitution of my country, symptoms of it must have been perceived in our frequent interviews. But you know that neither politics nor religion were ever the subjects of our conversations. Philosophy engrossed us wholly.

Politicians may think there are no objects of any consequence besides those which immediately interest *them*; but objects far superior to any of which they have an idea engaged our attention, and the discussion of them was accompanied with a satisfaction to which they are strangers. Happy would it be for the world if their pursuits were as tranquil, and their objects as innocent and as friendly to the best interests of mankind, as ours. It is, however, a noble consideration, that the order and final happiness of the universe will not be interrupted by anything that they can devise or do, while there is one Infinite Mind superintending all things, and bringing good out of, and by means of, all the evil that they can contrive or produce.

In the character of a minister of religion I never appeared with *you*, but as such (now that I am perhaps taking my final leave of you) permit me, though in religious persuasion differing from you all, to commit you to the protection and blessing of that Great Being, *whose we are, and whom*, I trust, *we all serve*, and who established that course of nature which is the object of our common investigation ; and when we meet, as I doubt not we shall, in another state, may the meeting be most happy !

With the greatest esteem and affection, I am, my valued friends, sincerely yours, JOSEPH PRIESTLEY.

CHAPTER VIII

MRS. "SKIM"

AMONG Mr. Galton's children were a son who caused a stir in the world and a daughter who caused a stir in the family. The son, Samuel Tertius, married Erasmus Darwin's daughter, Violetta, and one of their children was Francis Galton. The daughter, Mary Anne, married a Dutch gentleman named Schimmelpenninck, and wrote an autobiography which outraged her relations. A copy of this work is in the present writer's possession; it belonged to Sir Francis Galton, and his pencilled comments on certain passages appear in the margins.

One of these comments (never of course meant for publication) sums up the attitude of her family so exactly that it must be quoted. Apparently she and her husband took the management of the property she inherited from her grandfather out of her father's hands. In her *Life* it is stated that her mother took offence at this, and thenceforward she was estranged from her family. Here is Sir Francis Galton's marginal comment:

" As though this was the only matter! Demon of mischief-making, whose name was rarely mentioned by any of the family, and then only with horror!—winning confidences and then misrepresenting friends to each other! She broke off *eleven* marriages."

It should be observed that Sir Francis Galton was by nature charitable and never prone to emphasis or over-statement. His comment may therefore be accepted as the kindest and mildest view taken of his aunt by any member of the family.

In biography an omission is often equivalent to a distortion. For this reason it is necessary to record that Mrs. Schimmelpenninck (called "Skim" for short by her relations) was disliked and distrusted by her entire family. She, no doubt, returned the compliment and did not trouble to mince matters when she wrote her memories of Dr. Darwin, who was beloved and revered by her parents, brothers, and sisters. Her portrait of him was considered an outrage by Darwins and Galtons alike, and "Aunt Skim" became a sort of family Guy Fawkes. We must also bear in mind that she was between ten and fourteen years of age when the doctor impressed her in the way she has recorded, and that his sayings were recollected in tranquillity at the age of seventy-five.

Clearly she hated him and everything he stood for. But hatred is not a bad guide to one aspect of the truth; and in spite of her general reputation for mendacity, in spite of her youth when she knew him and her age when she wrote about him, in spite even of her spite, her portrait of the doctor is so manifestly sincere, from one particular angle so true to life, that the substantial accuracy of the representation cannot be questioned.

Mrs. "Skim" belonged to that not uncommon type of person who is obsessed by the questions of sin, atonement, repentance, punishment, and the entire repertory of disturbing theological features that made life so exciting for John Bunyan. Pages of analysis could not place her before the reader more vividly than one passage from her autobiography. When she was a child, she declares, the novels of Fielding and Smollett "desecrated the library shelves . . . their evil influences I can never forget; and I think with horror of this pestilential literature, and of its deleterious effect both on myself and on those under whose care I was placed. . . . How great an obligation do we owe to Sir Walter Scott for raising the tone of light literature, and infusing into it, not only much instruction and information, but noble and elevated sentiments, and a tone of feeling honourable, manly, highly moral, and to a certain degree Christian!"

The operative clause in the foregoing is " to a certain degree." It suggests the reservation of a sectarian; and when she wrote it Mrs. "Skim," having passed through all the emotional crises that usually precede permanent plantation on the impregnable rock of truth, was a Moravian. She was in fact a very pious woman; but in spite of her piety, there is no reason to doubt her veracity.

Questions of right and wrong were racking her conscience when, at the age of ten, she first caught sight of Dr. Darwin. Let her speak for herself:

" I was thus in a state of mind to receive evil from a new and hurtful influence which now approached our family circle.

" It was in the course of that autumn (1788) that

the celebrated Dr. Darwin first came to see my mother at Barr. His arrival was an era in my life; I saw him then with the eyes of a child, and now, in age, I can only describe him from the stores I then locked up in my memory.

" It was in the latter part of the morning that a carriage drove up to our door, of that description then called a ' Sulky,' because calculated to hold one person only. The carriage was worn, and bespattered with mud. Lashed on the place appropriated to the boot in ordinary carriages was a large pail for the purpose of watering the horses, together with some hay and oats beside it. In the top of the carriage was a skylight, with an awning which could at pleasure be drawn over; this was for the purpose of giving light to the doctor, who wrote most of his works on scraps of paper with a pencil as he travelled.

" The front of the carriage within was occupied by a receptacle for writing-paper and pencils, likewise for a knife, fork, and spoon; on one side was a pile of books reaching from the floor to nearly the front window of the carriage; on the other, a hamper containing fruit and sweetmeats, cream and sugar, great part of which, however, was demolished during the time the carriage traversed the forty miles which separated Derby from Barr. We all hastened to the parlour window, to see Dr. Darwin, of whom we had heard so much, and whom I was prepared to honour and venerate, in no common degree, as the restorer of my mother's health. What then was my astonishment at beholding him as he slowly got out of the carriage! His figure was vast and massive, his head was almost buried on his shoulders, and he wore a scratch wig, as it was then called, tied up in a little bob-tail behind. A habit of stammering made the closest attention necessary, in order to understand what he said. Meanwhile, amidst all this, the doctor's eye was deeply sagacious, the most so I think of any eye I remember ever to have seen; and I can conceive that no patient consulted Dr. Darwin who, so far as intelligence was concerned, was not inspired with confidence in beholding him: his observation was most keen; he constantly detected disease, from his sagacious observation of symptoms apparently so slight as to be unobserved by other doctors. His horror of fermented liquors, and his belief in the advantages both of eating largely, and eating an almost immeasurable abundance of sweet things, was well known to all his friends; and we had on this occasion, as indeed was the custom whenever he came, a luncheon-table set out with hothouse fruit, and West India sweetmeats, clotted cream, Stilton cheese, &c. When the whole party were settled at table, and I had lost the fear that the doctor would speak to me, and when, by dint of attention, I could manage to understand what he said, I was astonished at his wit, his anecdotes, and most entertaining conversation. I was particularly amused by anecdotes he told of his patients. There was one lady, the Duchess of D——, whom he had recently been called to attend, who was perishing, he said, under the effect of the white enamel paint which some ladies were then very fond of applying. The doctor at once perceived the cause of her malady, but he knew it would be tender ground to touch upon, since her use of the cosmetic was kept a profound secret, even from her family; he therefore put on a very grave face, and said she was certainly poisoned, asked if she had had her servants long, and if she had reason to think they owed her ill-will; he then said he should make the strictest examination of all the kitchen utensils, which he did; no satisfaction could be obtained. He then informed her Grace that poison might be absorbed by the skin as well as received by the stomach; had she observed the dyes of her gloves? &c., &c. At last, the Duchess of D——, after a great struggle, confessed she used the white lead enamel. It was soon removed. Dr. Darwin's ingenuity furnished her with some vegetable cosmetic in its stead; and her Grace completely recovered.

"With this, and various other anecdotes, did Dr. Darwin beguile the time whilst the dishes in his vicinity were rapidly emptied; but what was my astonishment when, at the end of the three hours during which the meal had lasted, he expressed his joy at hearing the dressing-bell, and hoped dinner would soon be announced. At last, to my sorrow, he discovered me, and said, 'I will now see if you are a clever and industrious little girl; translate me these lines of Virgil,' on which he began, no doubt, to repeat them, but to me, who could not even understand his English, they were wholly unintelligible. He then quoted some Greek lines, of which language I knew not a word, so that I got into great disgrace with him. This is the recollection of my first childish impressions

of Dr. Darwin; an eventful day, not only for myself,
was that which first introduced him to our family
circle."

A few months later the " hurtful influence " again
made itself felt.

" It was in the beginning of 1789 that my mother
was again far from well, and my father sent for Dr.
Darwin. Baneful and ominous these visits appeared
to me, and I felt an instinctive dread of them, child as
I was, for which I could assign no reason. All the
winter I had been more or less under the upward
aspiration I have described; and when on Dr. Darwin's
arrival, he entered the room and sat down to the usual
well-spread table which had been provided for him, I
felt an instant repulsion. His whole conversation, I
remember, on that occasion, was characterized by the
merriment and so-called wit which aimed its perpetual
shafts against those holy truths which, imperfectly
though I yet knew them, afforded me the only comfort in distress which I had ever experienced, and
seemed to me the only wells of living water in the
desert where we then found ourselves."

(A momentary pause, while we recall the fact that
she is still ten years old.)

" When I observed Dr. Darwin lingering over his
repast, and recollected my mother's suffering state, and
the high eulogiums with which she always spoke of
him, and her care to maintain his honour and to
consult his comfort, I was struck equally with aversion
and indignation at conduct which appeared to me to
evince a total want of feeling. I do not give this as a

judgment upon Dr. Darwin; perhaps, so far as his jocose manner extended, he might imagine it an alleviation in our care, but on me, a child, the impression was indelible. I could not admit the possibility of his allowing any idea to intervene between his entrance into the house and his ascertaining my mother's state and trying to relieve her. I will mention one observation of Dr. Darwin's, to show how grievous it is to receive objections to Holy Scripture without first looking round and ascertaining if there be not a reply. He said on one occasion that the Scriptures of the Old Testament were a tissue of fables, unworthy to be trusted even by their own confession, seeing it was there stated that the Book of the Law was lost for a long period, and only found again in the reign of Josiah. This staggered me not a little, for he omitted to add that this applied only to the original identical copy of the Law, since every king of Judah was obliged to transcribe a perfect copy upon his ascending the throne; that copies in like manner were deposited in every Levitical city, and that so exact were they in point of correctness, that the failure of one letter cancelled the sheet. Though I shrank with horror from such observations, and the sneering manner which accompanied them, and though they seemed to strengthen my resolution in the opposite direction, yet I believe from experience that it is wise not even to listen to things we know to be false, whether against the Holy Scripture, or against the character of individuals; for though we may rebut them at the time, yet often in hours of weakness or particular temptation, those very things will recur again, and insensibly obtain a lodgment even in the mind which had at first unhesitatingly rejected them. Well has the word of God compared the arguments of infidels to thorns and thistles; like the former, how do they lacerate and entangle the mind—or at least, as it were, catch the intellect or habits or tastes, which are the mind's clothing—and impede it; whilst, on the other hand, the sneers and gibes of the infidel, like the worthless thistledown, from their very lightness are wafted far and near, and soon grow up into a crop of poisonous weeds."

These were solemn thoughts. And the devil of it was that the "worthless thistledown" continued to be "wafted." About two years later the terrible doctor was called in to see Mary Anne's cousin, and left such an indelible impression on Mary Anne that, sixty-three years after, she still seemed "to see Dr. Darwin sitting on the sofa, as he gazed with almost a sneer on the beauty before him, beauty not merely physical, but yet more moral and intellectual; and never shall I forget the contrast between his figure and the fragile form of my cousin, who, as his patient, sat next him; fragile, indeed, she appeared, as though a breath might annihilate her; and yet there was that about her which seemed as a panoply of Divine strength, and before which the shafts of Dr. Darwin's wit against Divine truth, aimed cautiously at first, but afterwards more openly, recoiled innocuous. 'My dear madam,' said he, 'you have but one complaint; it is one ladies are very subject to, and it is the worst of all complaints;

and that is, having a conscience. Do get rid of it with all speed; few people have health or strength enough to keep such a luxury, for utility I cannot call it.'

"One of the party having expressed the hope that one day he would receive Christianity, he replied, 'Before I do that, you Christians must all be agreed. The other morning I received two parcels: one contained a work of Dr. Priestley's, proving there is no spirit, the other a work by Berkeley, Bishop of Cloyne, proving there is no matter. What am I to believe amongst you all?' I never shall forget the look with which this was said.

"On another occasion during my cousin's visit, the lady whom I designate as ' cousin Sally,' and who was much attached to her, said to Dr. Darwin, 'But, doctor, you will surely allow dear Priscilla to read religious books?' To which the doctor replied, ' My dear madam, toss them every one into the fire. I cannot permit one of them, excepting Quarles's *Emblems*, which may make her laugh.'"

It is becoming clear why there was no love lost between Darwin and Johnson. Mrs. "Skim" makes no comment on the humorous qualities of Quarles's *Emblems*. She may not have read it; on the other hand, she may have read it and laughed at it. One inclines to the former supposition. But she hasn't finished with Dr. Darwin yet:

"My mother's health was by no means fully re-established, so that in the course of that year and the next Dr. Darwin frequently visited us. I cannot answer for the exact period at which the incidents I shall mention took place, but I give them here as they occur to my memory. One observation, justice and truth, with Christian charity, call upon me to make. Let it be remembered that I am writing my own biography, not Dr. Darwin's. I am, therefore, describing not his character, but the impression he made upon me. The baleful impression made on my principles, habits, and feelings, by intercourse with that society, of which he, at that time, was the culminating point, was too powerful to be lightly passed over. I feel it a deep debt I owe to society to point out an evil, in the effects of which I was so long and woefully entangled.

"When I remember how lightly many persons are accustomed to speak, how lightly they allow themselves to say, colloquially, that which they would not fully sanction when in earnest, I would not record these painful characteristics of Dr. Darwin's conversation were not my motive to show the great power of casual influences over the minds of children, whether for good or evil.

"When I consider the effect of many of these things on myself, I seem to understand the awful warning that for every ' idle word ' we shall give an account. By ' idle,' I understand the lightest word which spreads evil around, however sunny or soft the air that bears it, but I do not understand by it the beautiful and sportive flower that gives fragrance and grace to the solid rock it garlands.

"Dr. Darwin often used to say, ' Man is an eating

animal, a drinking animal, and a sleeping animal, and
one placed in a material world, which alone furnishes
all the human animal can desire. He is gifted besides
with knowing faculties, practically to explore and to
apply the resources of this world to his use. These
are realities. All else is nothing; conscience and sentiment are mere figments of the imagination. Man has
but five gates of knowledge, the five senses; he can
know nothing but through them; all else is a vain
fancy, and as for the being of a God, the existence of a
soul, or a world to come, who can know anything
about them? Depend upon it, my dear madam,
these are only the bugbears by which men of sense
govern fools; nothing is real that is not an object of
sense.'

" As I heard these things, and remembered the high
esteem in which Dr. Darwin's talents were held, and
the respect with which his dicta were listened to, my
mind seemed shaken to its centre. I felt perplexed
and bewildered. . . ."

It certainly must have been very perplexing to a child
of twelve, though perhaps not more bewildering than
the contradictions of the Christian creeds.

Mrs. " Skim " goes on to tell us of the enthusiastic
reception accorded Darwin's *Botanic Garden* at Barr.
They were all rapturous over it. The doctor, she
says, gave as his reason for publishing the second
part before the first that it " was well to put the best
foot foremost." Her own admiration for the poem
was qualified by the feeling that it was too earthy—
" there is everything to fix the eye below, on what is

transient and mutable; nothing to raise it above, to the permanent and immutable; there is all in it to delight the eye or ear, nothing to touch the well-springs of the heart." And, curiously enough, she quotes the 19th Psalm as evidence of Darwin's irreligion. Had she read his *Zoonomia* she would have been surprised to find that he quoted the same verses in support of his religion.

"It so happened," she continues, "that Dr. Darwin paid us a visit shortly after the publication of the first volume of his work, and in the midst of its success. He told us that his bookseller . . . offered him for the copyright, or for the edition (I forget which), a sum at the rate of ten shillings a line. This was said amidst our large family party, our Oscott friends being present.

"On another occasion, my dear mother said to him, 'I was much pleased, doctor, with your magnificent description of the Upas; but I was also much surprised, and more especially at the notes containing an elaborate account of it, for I had always considered what we heard of the Upas as a myth.' The doctor laughingly replied, 'And so do I, my dear madam. There is not one word of truth in it; but so long as I can get the public to believe me, by dint not only of my own poetry, but also by the notes of my ingenious friend, and as every line puts ten shillings in my pocket, I shall go on *ad infinitum*, as haply the monks of old did with their equally true saintly legends.'—One good effect these things had upon me. They made me think that Dr. Darwin did not value truth, and I hence received, from his own lips, a salutary caution, and a standard by which to measure his dicta on other subjects."

It is nice to know that Dr. Darwin's conversation had at any rate " one good effect " on the harassed soul of Mrs. " Skim."

CHAPTER IX

DOMESTIC MATTERS

ONE of his sons said that Dr. Darwin had a strong antipathy to " personal questions " and never told his children anything about the earlier part of his life, when he was practising as a doctor in Lichfield. His biographer cannot respect his reticence. The little that is known about his private life must now be recorded.

He married, as we have seen, a girl of eighteen named Mary Howard. They had five children, two of whom died in infancy. After thirteen years of married life, and a long and painful illness, she died in 1770. They were very happy together and she was tenderly nursed by her husband throughout her rather delicate life, which was probably shortened by what Anna Seward calls " the frequency of her maternal situation during the first five years of her marriage." Within a few days of her death, she spoke of her married life to her friends; and if her confession sounds a trifle over-pitched to modern ears, we must not forget that it comes to us through the medium of Sewardese.

" Do not weep for my impending fate. In the short term of my life, a great deal of happiness has been comprised. The maladies of my frame were peculiar; the pains in my head and stomach, which no medicine could eradicate, were spasmodic and violent; and required stronger measures to render them supportable while they lasted, than my constitution could sustain without injury. The periods of exemption from these pains were frequently of several days duration, and in my intermissions I felt no indication of malady. Pain taught me the value of ease, and I enjoyed it with a glow of spirit seldom perhaps felt by the habitually healthy. While Dr. Darwin combated and assuaged my disease from time to time, his indulgence to all my wishes, his active desire to see me amused and happy, proved incessant. His house, as you know, has ever been the resort of people of science and merit. If, from my husband's great and extensive practice, I had much less of his society than I wished, yet the conversation of his friends, and of my own, was ever ready to enliven the hours of his absence. As occasional malady made me doubly enjoy health, so did those frequent absences give a zest, even to delight, when I could be indulged with his company. My three boys have ever been docile and affectionate. Children as they are, I could trust them with important secrets, so sacred do they hold every promise they make. They scorn deceit and falsehood of every kind, and have less selfishness than generally belongs to childhood. Married to any other man, I do not suppose I could have lived a third part of those years which I have passed with Dr. Darwin; he has prolonged my days, and he has blessed them.''

Darwin's intense professional activity during the years he was at Lichfield must have had an unfortunate effect upon his three sons. At the end of the day he was utterly fagged out and quite incapable of the patience necessary in dealing with children. His own views on bringing up children are interesting at this point. "If you would not have your children arrogant, conceited, and hypocritical," he says, "do not let them perceive that you are continually watching and attending to them; nor can you keep that perpetual watch *without* their perceiving it. Inspire them with a disdain of meanness, falsehood, and promise-breaking; but do not try to effect this purpose by precept and declamation, but, as occasion rises, by expressed contempt of such as commit those faults, whether it be themselves or others. Teach them benevolence and industry by your own example, for children are emulous to acquire the habits of advanced life, and attach to them an idea of dignity and importance."

He also declares that "reprimands and even admonitions should be always applied in private, but applause or reward in public." Emulation he thinks harmful because it causes envy; and in his opinion a love of credit and an apprehension of shame is "not the true source whence our actions ought to spring, which should be from our duty to others and ourselves." He considers that sympathy with the pains and pleasures of others is the foundation of all our social virtues, that it can best be inculcated by example and the expression of our own sympathy, and that "compassion or sympathy with the pains of others, ought also to extend to the brute creation . . . to destroy even insects wantonly shows an unreflecting mind or a depraved heart." On the other hand he is strongly opposed to mere sentiment. "Children," he asserts, "should be taught in their early education to feel for all the remediable evils which they observe in others; but they should at the same time be taught sufficient firmness of mind not entirely to destroy their own happiness by their sympathizing with too great sensibility with the numerous irremediable evils which exist in the present system of the world: as by indulging that kind of melancholy they decrease the sum total of public happiness, which is so far rather reprehensible than commendable."

These are some of his views on the moral education of children. His method of imparting them to his own children was peculiar at that time. He used irony, not the rod, when he wished to correct them; but his irony cut like a whip. He was despotic and frequently contemptuous; and though later on, when his professional struggles were less severe, he showed much affection for them, it is doubtful whether they ever forgot the early effect of his "resistless sarcasms."

His eldest son, Charles, inherited his love of science and not a few of his other characteristics, including his stammer. He, too, went to study medicine at Edinburgh, where he made many friends and won the first gold medal of the Æsculapian Society for "having discovered a criterion by which *pus* may be distinguished from *mucus*." While he was in his twenty-first year he dissected the brain of a child, cut his finger during the operation, and died as a result of the wound. His father reached Edinburgh before he died, and when it

was all over wrote letters to Wedgwood and his youngest
son Robert in which he gave vent to the anguish of his
mind. He felt the death of this boy deeply, and nearly
three years later referred to his distress as though it
were of quite recent occurrence.

The second son, Erasmus, was unlike his father in
almost every respect. His disposition was quiet and
retiring. He was a numismatist, a genealogist, and a
statistician. He was also a dreamer, who forgot to
pay his debts and forgot to claim his credits, who
suffered from "defect of voluntary power," and lived
listlessly from day to day. He had a gentle and
extremely sensitive nature, which attracted Thomas
Day. At first he wanted to take holy orders, but his
father made caustic remarks relative to the indolence and
effeminacy of the clergy, and he became a lawyer. The
doctor was not kind to this son. The lad's dreamy,
retiring, sensitive spirit shrank from the parent's biting
sarcasms, and it is possible he never got over the early
suppression of his religious instincts. Eventually he
settled in Derby, where he did fairly well. But the
keeping of accounts was always a painful business to
him, and his affairs gradually became so entangled that
one cold and stormy December evening he walked
down to the bottom of his garden and flung himself
into the River Derwent. His body was not recovered
till the following morning.

When the news of his disappearance was brought to
his father, the doctor went down to the river and
stood there for a long time in great agony of mind.
Emma, one of his daughters by his second marriage,

tells us what happened when the news was brought next day that the body had been found. "He immediately got up, but staggered so much that Violetta and I begged of him to sit down, which he did, and leaned his head upon his hand . . . he was exceedingly agitated, and did not speak for many minutes. His first words were, 'I beg you will not, any of you, ask to see your poor brother's corpse'; and upon our assuring him that we had not the least wish to do so, he soon after said that this was the greatest shock he had felt since the death of his poor Charles."

In a letter to his son Robert the same day he says: "I write in great anguish of mind to acquaint you with a dreadful event." And soon after he tells Robert that a monument is to be erected to his brother, adding: "Mrs. Darwin and I intend to lie in Breadsall church by his side."

This third son, Robert, who became the father of Charles Darwin, was also sensitive to an abnormal degree; and as a remarkable memory was one of his chief endowments, the doctor's biting tongue and imperious nature left an abiding impression on him. He, too, became a doctor, but hated his profession because it constantly brought suffering before his eyes. His chief pleasure in life was to see people enjoying themselves, and he did his utmost to make everyone round him happy. His father took him to Shrewsbury before he was twenty-one, and gave him £20, saying, "Let me know when you want more, and I will send it you." But in spite of his dislike of doctoring Robert did well and soon had a large practice in and about Shrewsbury.

His memories of his father, though few, are valuable. He tells us that the doctor possessed great facility in explaining any difficult subject, he himself attributing this power to his habit of always talking about whatever he was studying, "turning and moulding the subject according to the capacity of his hearers." He remembered the doctor saying that "the world is not governed by the clever men, but by the active and energetic"; and on another occasion that "common sense would be improving when men left off wearing as much flour on their heads as would make a pudding, when women left off wearing rings in their ears, like savages wear nose-rings, and when fire-grates were no longer made of polished steel." The doctor had little use for another item of female adornment, and called it "that coat of mail, the whale-bone stays."

We also learn from Robert that his father was naturally of "a bold disposition, but that a succession of accidents made a deep impression on his mind, and that he became very cautious. When he was about five years old he received an accidental blow on the top of his head, sufficiently severe to give him a white lock of hair for life. Later on, when he was fishing with his brothers, they put him into a bag with only his feet out, and thus being blinded he walked into the river, and was very nearly drowned. Again, when he and Lord George Cavendish were playing with gunpowder at school, it exploded, and he was badly injured; and lastly, he broke his kneecap."

The doctor was kind and considerate to his servants. Once, when Robert owed him a small sum of money, he told him to buy a goose-pie with it, for which Shrewsbury was then famous, and send it at Christmas to an old woman living in Birmingham, "for she, as you may remember, was your nurse, which is the greatest obligation, if well performed, that can be received from an inferior." Robert also notes that his father "was sometimes violent in his anger, but his sympathy and benevolence soon made him try to soothe or soften matters." Incidentally, Edgeworth admitted that he had seen the doctor angry "five or six times . . . but then the motive never was personal. When Dr. Darwin beheld any example of inhumanity or injustice, he never could refrain his indignation. . . . If a friend was ever hurt by a heedless shaft of his wit, he poured balm into the wound by the kindest expressions of sympathy and regret."

The doctor kept up a good correspondence with his son Robert. Here are some characteristic passages in his letters:

I am sorry to hear you say you have many enemies, and one enemy often does much harm.   The best way, when any little slander is told one, is never to make any piquant or angry answer ; as the person who tells you what another says against you always tells them in return what you say of them.   I used to make it a rule always to receive all such information very coolly, and never to say anything biting against them which could go back again ; and by these means many who were once averse to me in time became friendly.   Dr. Small always went and drank tea with those whom he heard had spoken against him ; and it is best to show a little attention at public assemblies to those who dislike one ; and it generally conciliates them. . . .

I think you and I should sometimes exchange a long medical letter, especially when any uncommon diseases occur ; both as it improves one in writing clear, intelligible English and preserves instructive cases. . . . Now in medicine I am sure, unless one reads the work of others, one is liable perpetually to copy one's *own* prescriptions, and methods of treatment ; till one's whole practice is but an imitation of oneself, and half a score medicines make up one's whole materia medica, and the apothecaries say the doctor has but four or five prescriptions to cure all diseases. . . .

As to fees, if your business pays you well on the whole, I would not be uneasy about making absolutely the most of it. To live comfortably all one's life is better than to make a very large fortune towards the end of it. . . .

There are two kinds of covetousness, one the fear of poverty, the other the desire of gain. The former, I believe, at some times affects all people who live by a profession. . . .

After he had left Lichfield, Robert wrote asking for his advice concerning a young fellow whom he wished to see well started as an apothecary. The doctor replied:

I cannot give any letters of recommendation to Lichfield, as I am and have been from their infancy acquainted with all the apothecaries there ; and as such letters must be directed to some of their patients, they would both feel and resent it. . . .

I should advise your friend to use at first all means to get acquainted with the people of all ranks. At first a parcel of blue and red glasses at the windows might gain part of the retail business on market-days, and thus get acquaintance with that class of people. I remember Mr. Green of Lichfield, who is now growing very old, once told me his retail business, by means of his show-shop and many-coloured

windows, produced him £100 a year.   Secondly, I remember
a very foolish, garrulous apothecary at Cannock, who had
great business without any knowledge or even art, except that
he persuaded people he kept good drugs ; and this he accomplished by only one stratagem, and that was by *boring* every
person who was so unfortunate as to step into his shop with
the goodness of his drugs.   " Here 's a fine piece of assa-
fœtida, smell of this valerian, taste this album græcum.   Dr.
Fungus says he never saw such a fine piece in his life."   Thirdly,
dining every market day at a farmer's ordinary would bring
him some acquaintance, and I don't think a little impediment
in his speech would at all injure him, but rather the contrary
by attracting notice.   Fourthly, card assemblies—I think at
Lichfield surgeons are not admitted as they are here—but they
are to dancing assemblies ; these therefore he should attend.
Thus have I emptied my quiver of the *arts* of the Pharmacopol.
Dr. K——d, I think, supported his business by perpetual
boasting, like a Charlatan ; this does for a blackguard character, but ill suits a more polished or modest man. . . .
I will certainly send to him when first I go to Lichfield. . . .

After the death of his first wife, Dr. Darwin, who
was not cut out for a celibate, solaced himself with the
society of a lady whose name may or may not have
been Parker.   His immediate legitimate descendants
suppressed all details concerning her, though they were
unable to suppress the fact of the connection because
the doctor himself made no bones about it.   He not
only acknowledged his two illegitimate daughters, but
had them well educated, started a school for them at
Ashbourne in Derbyshire, wrote a pamphlet on Female
Education for their benefit, sent his daughters by his
second wife to the school, and influenced many of his
friends to do the same.   The two Misses Parker, as they

were called, constantly stayed with him, were treated as members of his family, and became very popular in Derby. One of them eventually married Mr. Hadley, the leading surgeon there.

It was between his first and second marriage that Anna Seward made several onslaughts on the doctor's heart. Anna's book on the doctor got her into hot water with the family, and even Charles Darwin accused her of " scandalous negligence." But Charles went too far when he described her style of writing as " disagreeable " and " nauseous." Possibly that is how it affected the Victorians, but it affects us in quite a different way. Both her style and her sentiments are richly entertaining and the person who cannot enjoy them is to be pitied.

Edgeworth makes it clear that she was in love with the doctor even during his first marriage, and Robert Darwin wrote to her: "Were I to have published my father's papers . . . some circumstances must unavoidably have appeared, which would have been as unpleasant for you to read as for me to publish." Which can only be taken in one way.

The doctor, who loved the society of women and must have revelled in hers, probably had no objection to a little flirtation now and then, but whenever Anna's conversation began to take on the style of her correspondence, he quickly changed his tone. One is not surprised to learn, from Anna herself, that she possessed no serious letters from him—only a trivial note or so —and there is not a little pique in her description of him, which includes this most revealing passage:

" While on abstracted themes his imagination glowed; while on entrance and on commencing a conversation, his countenance wore a benevolent smile, we invariably found, on its progress, a cold satiric atmosphere around him, repulsing all attempts to interchange the softer sympathies of friendship."

If we substitute " I " for " we," and lay all the emphasis on the last ten words, we have here a valuable sidelight on the Darwin-Seward amorosities.

The doctor had, of course, known Anna as a child. " He became a sort of poetic preceptor to me in my early youth," she confesses; " if I have critical knowledge in my favourite science, I hold myself chiefly indebted for it to him." Anna was certainly capable of appreciating great poetry—" she lisped Milton's numbers " at the age of three—but she had an almost infallible appreciation of tenth-rate verse. In this respect she only drew the line at the poetry of Mrs. Charlotte Smith, the "Swan" of Bignor, which received the following eulogium in the *Gentleman's Magazine* of that time: " It is trifling praise for Mrs. Smith's sonnets to pronounce them superior to Shakespeare's and Milton's." The " Swan " of Lichfield not only described Mrs. Smith's sonnets as " lamentables," but called her sister-Swan a pea-hen; and, referring to the contemporary praise of Mrs. Smith, so far forgot her style as to say, " It makes one sick!"

Anna's own poetry was praised by everyone except her father, who, ever since Darwin told him that his daughter's poetry was better than his, became a little restive whenever the subject cropped up. Darwin undoubtedly encouraged her, and she gives us several examples of the easy, familiar terms they were on together. Here is one:

He was not in the habit of throwing his imagination into his letters ; they were rather hurried over as tasks than written *con amore*. I have often heard him say he did not possess the epistolary graces. He told me one day, when I was about six or seven and twenty, that he wished to write to Dr. Franklin, to compliment him upon having united modern science and philosophy ; and desired I would put his thoughts into my own language. He took his pen, and throwing on paper the heads of what he purposed saying, desired I would give them verbal ornament, and that he would call next day for the result. He did call ; and, looking over what I had written, laughingly commended the style ; copied the manuscript verbatim in my presence, directed that copy to Dr. Franklin, America, and sent it instantly to the post-office by my father's servant. . . . He said he felt inclined to make a still more flattering superscription, "Dr. Franklin, the World." . . .

Franklin got the letter all right and replied to it. " I hope," wrote Darwin to Wedgwood, " Dr. Franklin will live to see peace, to see America recline under her own vine and fig-tree, turning her swords into plough-shares, &c."

Darwin started a botanical society in Lichfield, but it never numbered more than three members, including himself. He did something else in connection with botany, to which no pen but Miss Seward's can do justice:

" About the year 1777, Dr. Darwin purchased a little,

wild, umbrageous valley, a mile from Lichfield, amongst the only rocks which neighbour that city so nearly. It was irriguous from various springs, and swampy from their plenitude. A mossy fountain, of the purest and coldest water imaginable, had, near a century back, induced the inhabitants of Lichfield to build a cold bath in the bosom of the vale. *That*, till the doctor took it into his possession, was the only mark of human industry which could be found in the tangled and sequestered scene.

"One of its native features had long excited the attention of the curious; a rock, which, in the central depth of the glen, drops perpetually, about three times in a minute. Aquatic plants border its top and branch from its fissures. No length of summer drought abates, no rains increase its humidity, no frost congeals its droppings. The doctor cultivated this spot—
' And Paradise was open'd in the wild.'

"In some parts he widened the brook into small lakes, that mirrored the valley; in others, he taught it to wind between shrubby margins. Not only with trees of various growth did he adorn the borders of the fountain, the brook, and the lakes, but with various classes of plants, uniting the Linnæan science with the charm of landscape. . . ."

"Dr. Darwin restrained his friend Miss Seward's steps to this, her always favourite scene, till it had assumed its new beauties from cultivation. He purposed accompanying her on her first visit to his botanic garden, but a medical summons into the country deprived her of that pleasure. She took her tablets and pencil, and, seated on a flower-bank, in the midst of that luxuriant retreat, wrote the following lines, while the sun was gilding the glen, and while birds, of every plume, poured their song from the boughs. . . .

O, come not here, ye Proud, whose breasts infold
Th' insatiate wish of glory, or of gold ;
O come not ye, whose branded foreheads wear
Th' eternal frown of envy, or of care ;
For you no Dryad decks her fragrant bowers,
For you her sparkling urn no Naiad pours ;
Unmark'd by you light Graces skim the green,
And hovering Cupids aim their shafts unseen.

But, thou ! whose mind the well-attemper'd ray
Of Taste, and Virtue, lights with purer day ;
Whose finer sense each soft vibration owns,
Mute and unfeeling to discorded tones ;
Like the fair flower that spreads its lucid form
To meet the sun, but shuts it to the storm ;
For thee my borders nurse the glowing wreath,
My fountains murmur, and my zephyrs breathe ;
My painted birds their vivid plumes unfold,
And insect armies wave their wings of gold.

And if with thee some hapless maid should stray,
Disastrous love companion of her way,
O lead her timid step to yonder glade,
Whose weeping rock incumbent alders shade !
There, as meek evening wakes the temperate breeze,
And moonbeams glimmer through the trembling trees,
The rills, that gurgle round, shall sooth her ear,
The weeping rock shall number tear for tear ;
And as sad Philomel, alike forlorn,
Sings to the night, reclining on her thorn,

While, at sweet intervals, each falling note
Sighs in the gale, and whispers round the grot,
The sister-woe shall calm her aching breast,
And softest slumbers steal her cares to rest.

Thus spoke the Genius [1] as he stept along,
And bade these lawns to Peace and Truth belong ;
Down the steep slopes he led, with modest skill,
The grassy pathway and the vagrant rill ;
Stretch'd o'er the marshy vale the willowy mound,
Where shines the lake amid the cultur'd ground ;
Rais'd the young woodland, smooth'd the wavy green,
And gave to Beauty all the quiet scene.

O ! may no ruder step these bowers prophane,
No midnight wassailers deface the plain ;
And when the tempests of the wintry day
Blow golden autumn's varied leaves away,
Winds of the North, restrain your icy gales,
Nor chill the bosom of these HALLOWED VALES!

" When Miss Seward gave this little poem to Dr.
Darwin, he seemed pleased with it and said, ' I shall
send it to the periodical publications; but it ought to
form the exordium of a great work. The Linnæan
system is unexplored poetic ground, and a happy
subject for the muse. It affords fine scope for poetic
landscape; it suggests metamorphoses of the Ovidian
kind, though reversed. Ovid made men and women
into flowers, plants, and trees. You should make
flowers, plants, and trees, into men and women. I,'
continued he, ' will write the notes, which must be
scientific; and you shall write the verse.' "

[1] By the Genius of the place is meant its first cultivator, Dr. Darwin.

Miss Seward objected that the " plan was not strictly proper for a female pen," but that it was eminently adapted to " the efflorescence of his own fancy." After a little friendly argument, it was decided that he should do it—and he did.

Anna is very definite on the subject of Darwin's repeated statement that he only wrote for money. "I have often smiled to hear him boast of his ' so much money per couplet,' conscious, as I was, that it was an artful way of telling us how highly his talents were rated. . . . Darwin would not have written meanly for any price that folly would have paid him for stooping his muse to her level." James Keir says the same thing: " The works of Dr. Darwin are a more faithful monument and more true mirror of his mind than can be said of those of most authors. He was not one of those who wrote . . . from any other incitement than the ardent love of the subject." Anna says that he had a very high opinion of his own work, but her view is contradicted by all his other friends. When an engraving of Wright's portrait of him was selling well, this is how he wrote to Robert: " The great honour of all is to have one's head upon a sign-post, unless, indeed, upon Temple Bar!"

Preserved in Darwin's Commonplace Book there is a long letter to him from Hutton, the founder of the science of geology, which, from its bantering tone, proves there was never any danger of the doctor suffering from swelled head. It also proves that, among his male acquaintances, the doctor was not averse from humour of the Rabelaisian order, though we may safely take Miss Seward's word for his decorum in the domestic circle: "I never," she says, "in his most gay and unconstrained moments, heard one indecent word, one indelicate equivoque proceed from the lips of Dr. Darwin."

In November, 1781, Anna Seward wrote to her friend Dr. Whalley that "Dr. Darwin left Lichfield only about eight months since. When he lived here, we two were the poets of the place. If Darwin chose to appear under that character, he would be one of the first of our time. *He* looks like a butcher, and *I* like a fat cook maid."

And a year later she wrote to the same friend:

Who do you think tapped at the dressing-room door, in about half an hour after you left it, and entered with a smiling countenance ?—who but Dr. Darwin, verily and indeed. He told me it was an age since he had seen me. I replied that I was happy to see him then, and did not even look a reproach for an absence so long and so unfriendly. But where my affections are tenderly interested, I must reproach before I can forgive. . . . I know well enough that Mr. Romney's art was the loadstone which drew hither that large mass of genius and sarcasm ; that he had heard of the picture and wished to see it. He saw it with seeming pleasure and very warm praise. Without affection enough to express, or feel resentment (ah ! we must at some time at least have believed ourselves beloved ere we can feel personal tenderness), I have yet that sort of regard for Dr. Darwin, as will always make me see him with pleasure when he looks willing to please. . . . He stayed till the 9 o'clock bell summoned us to go down and pass the remainder of the evening with my father. The doctor went, but Giovanni stayed. . . . Ah, need I name the subject of our conversation ? He set out for Coventry this morn, and does not return till Thursday. It was fortunate that the business of his profession, which takes him so often out of Lichfield, did not once snatch him away during the two swiftly flying hours of your residence here. Adieu! Adieu!

The picture referred to was one that Romney painted of Anna when she was staying with the Hayleys at Eartham in the summer of 1782. This letter is a pretty clear indication that Anna would have loved the doctor, if only he could have been induced to love her. . . .

In the spring of the year 1778 the children of Colonel Chandos Pole were nearly killed by the prescriptions of a Derby doctor, so their mother brought them to see Dr. Darwin. If Anna Seward had entertained any hopes that the doctor might, some time or other, become more to her than a "poetic preceptor," she must have done her best to forget them when Mrs. Pole arrived at Lichfield. But though Anna's heart sank, her pen did not lose its vigour. "Mrs. Pole," she informs us, "was then in the full bloom of her youth and beauty. Agreeable features; the glow of health; a fascinating smile; a fine form, tall and graceful; playful sprightliness of manners; a benevolent heart, and maternal affection in all its unwearied cares and touching tenderness, contributed to inspire Dr. Darwin's admiration, and to secure his esteem."

This is just Anna's stylish way of saying that the doctor fell head over ears in love with Mrs. Pole at first sight. Outwardly he remained calm and doctored the children, noting in his Commonplace Book, under the heading "Atrophy of Infants," that "Miss Milly Pole, about 3 years old, from a very healthy, lively, beautiful child, lost her spirits and flesh, without fever or tumid belly, or any apparent cause. She eats her meals and sleeps well, but will not stand on her feet. She has been gradually getting worse some weeks." He then theorizes on the whys and wherefores, remarks all the symptoms, gives her cold chicken and small beer, and eventually cures her with opium.

The grateful mother left Lichfield with her children's health and the doctor's heart. No sooner was she out of the house than he turned to poetry for solace, begging Mr. Boulton in eighteen rhymed couplets to make a beautiful "tea-vase" for his lady-love. That done, he gave himself up to melancholy, and addressed "proud Radburn" (Colonel Pole's residence) in a manner more becoming the admirer of a married woman:

> Farewell ! a long farewell !—your shades among
> No more these eyes shall drink Eliza's charms ;
> No more these ears the music of her tongue !—
> O ! doom'd for ever to another's arms !

But he was in luck. Only a few months later Mrs. Pole was down with a fever and he was sent for. One night she lay critically ill; but as he was not asked to stay in the house (Colonel Pole having probably observed symptoms of quite unprofessional anxiety in his manner towards the patient), he passed the hours till daybreak beneath the window of her bedroom, watching the shadows cast on the blind by the nurse or her husband as they went to and fro. His anxiety becoming unendurable, he relieved himself in verse, more distinguished for its metre than its merit.

Mrs. Pole's recovery impelled the doctor to address the River Derwent in eight picturesque stanzas, the last of which might have led to serious misunderstandings between himself and the colonel:

> And tell her, Derwent, as you murmur by,
> . How in these wilds with hopeless love I burn,
> Teach your lone vales and echoing caves to sigh,
> And mix my briny sorrows with your urn.

It was, perhaps, a fortunate day for poetry when Colonel Pole died. This happy event took place in 1780. The colonel was twice as old as his wife, and his temper, we are told, was "peevish and suspicious." He left her £600 a year and provision for their three children. Being a very attractive person, his widow was soon receiving the attentions of all the eligible young men in the neighbourhood. If the gossip of the match-makers could be trusted, there was little doubt that poor Darwin's love would continue to burn hopelessly. But the subject is a delicate one, and the help of Miss Seward must be invoked:

"Dr. Darwin soon, however, saw her surrounded by rivals, whose time of life had nearer parity with her own, yet in its summer bloom, while his age nearly approached its half century; whose fortunes were affluent and patrimonial, while his were professional; who were jocund bachelors, while he had children for whom he must provide. . . .

" Mrs. Pole, it has already been remarked, had much vivacity and sportive humour, with very engaging frankness of temper and manners. Early in her widowhood she was rallied in a large company upon Dr. Darwin's passion for her, and was asked what she would do with her captive philosopher. 'He is not very fond of churches, I believe, and if he would go there for my sake, I shall scarcely follow him. He is too old for me.' 'Nay, madam, what are fifteen years on the right side?' She replied, with an arch smile, 'I have had so *much* of that right side!'

" The confession was thought inauspicious to the doctor's hopes, but it did not prove so; the triumph of intellect was complete. Without that native perception and awakened taste for literary excellence, which the first Mrs. Darwin possessed, this lady became tenderly sensible of the flattering difference between the attachment of a man of genius, and wide celebrity, and that of young fox-hunting esquires, dashing militaries, and pedantic gownsmen; for she was said to have specimens of all these classes in her train. They could speak their own passion, but could not immortalize her charms. However benevolent, friendly, and sweet-tempered, she was not perhaps exactly the woman to have exclaimed with Akenside :

> Mind, mind alone, bear witness earth and heaven !
> The living fountain in itself contains
> Of beauteous and sublime !

" Yet did her choice support his axiom when she took Dr. Darwin for her husband. Darwin, never handsome, or personally graceful, with extremely impeded utterance; with hard features on a rough surface; older much in appearance than in reality; lame and clumsy!—and this, when half the wealthy youth of Derbyshire were said to have disputed the prize with him.''

But there were stipulations. She had, says Anna, taken a dislike to Lichfield—or possibly (who knows?) a dislike to Anna—and, in spite of the doctor's prayers, entirely declined to live there. The doctor was too much in love to put down his foot, and he went to Derby. '' His reputation and the unlimited confidence of the public followed him thither, and would have followed him to the metropolis, or to any provincial town, to which he might have chosen to remove.'' Anna could not resist a final fling at her '' low-brow '' rival and a last dig at the man who might so easily have married someone more on his own intellectual level. In 1785 she wrote to an acquaintance:

Almost five years are elapsed since Dr. Darwin left Lichfield. A handsome young widow, relict of Colonel Pole, by whom she had three children, drew from us, in the hymeneal chain, our celebrated physician, our poetic and witty friend.

The doctor was in love like a very Celadon, and a numerous young family are springing up in consequence of a union, which was certainly a little unaccountable ; not that there was any wonder that a fine, graceful, and affluent young woman, should fascinate a grave philosopher ; but that a sage of no elegant external, and sunk into the vale of years, should, by so gay a lady, be preferred to younger, richer, and handsomer suitors, was the marvel ; especially since, though lively, benevolent, and by no means deficient in native wit, she was never suspected of a taste for science, or works of imagination. Yet so it was ; and she makes her ponderous spouse a very attached, and indeed devoted wife ! The poetic philosopher, in return, transfers the amusement of his leisure hours, from the study of botany and mechanics, and the composition of odes, and heroic verses, to fabricating riddles and charades ! Thus employed, his mind is somewhat in the same predicament with Hercules's body, when he sat amongst the women, and handled the distaff. . . .

From a note in the handwriting of the doctor's second wife, preserved in the Commonplace Book, it is plain that " lettered elegance " was not her strong suit. Writing in a very unformed hand, rather as a girl of ten might write to-day, she made a list of her children by the doctor—in those days women could hardly be expected to remember all their children offhand—with the dates of their births. She recorded seven children born in the first nine years of their marriage. Three boys and three girls survived infancy, and the girls were famous for their beauty in the early years of the nineteenth century.

The doctor was adored by all the children of his second marriage (he was now no longer a struggling physician with a delicate wife), and Sir Francis Galton declared that his mother, Darwin's daughter Violetta, " never wearied of talking of him."

There is an interesting entry in the Commonplace Book, dated 31 January, 1782: " Mrs. Darwin was brought to bed in the morning. The child had a violent purging all the next night and perpetual crying, owing I suppose to its having been suckled by a woman of the parish, and taken much food too early, when it ought as yet to have had no food."

Is it possible that the second Mrs. Darwin refused to suckle her children? If so, she was partly responsible for these lines by her husband:

Connubial Fair ! whom no fond transport warms
To lull your infant in maternal arms ;
Who, bless'd in vain with tumid bosoms, hear
His tender wailings with unfeeling ear ;
The soothing kiss and milky rill deny
To the sweet pouting lips and glistening eye !—
Ah ! what avails the cradle's damask roof,
The eider bolster, and embroidered woof !
Oft hears the gilded couch unpitied plains,
And many a tear the tassel'd cushion stains!
No voice so sweet attunes his cares to rest,
So soft no pillow as his mother's breast !—
Thus charmed to sweet repose, when twilight hours
Shed their soft influence on celestial bowers,
The cherub Innocence, with smile divine,
Shuts his white wings, and sleeps on beauty's shrine.

CHAPTER X

THE DOCTOR

In the summer of 1778, the Countess of Northesk, accompanied by a friend and her daughter, Lady Carnegie, stopped a night at the chief inn of Lichfield. They were on their way to Scotland by the shortest possible route. The countess was dying of consumption and wanted to reach home before the event. She had been to see all the leading physicians of London and Bath, but they had been unable to check the progress of her disease and had told her to prepare for an early death. The landlady of the inn noted her wasted condition, the hectic flush in her cheeks, her laboured breathing, and said: " I wish, madam, that you would send for *our* doctor; he is so famous."

More from languor than from hope, the countess sent for Dr. Darwin. He came, saw that he could do nothing on a cursory examination, and begged her, with her daughter and friend, to stay with him as his guests for a fortnight. They accepted his invitation and were duly received at his house. One of the first things he did was to ask Miss Seward to visit his patient constantly, to keep her amused and prevent her from thinking too much of herself. Miss Seward noticed that whenever his patient was engrossed in the conversation, the doctor would sit "in meditative silence" closely observing her.

One evening, after quietly contemplating her for a considerable period, the doctor said:

"Lady Northesk, an art was practised in former years, which the medical world has very long disused; that of injecting blood into the veins by a syringe, and thus repairing the waste of diseases like yours. Human blood, and that of calves and sheep, were used promiscuously. Superstition attached impiety to the practice. It was put a stop to in England by a bull of excommunication from some of our popish princes, against the practitioners of sanguinary injection. That it had been practised with success, we may, from this interdiction, fairly conclude; else restraint upon its continuance must have been superfluous. We have a very ingenious watchmaker here, whom I think I could instruct to form a proper instrument for the purpose, if you chose to submit to the experiment."

The countess agreed; and Miss Seward offered to supply blood from her own veins for the necessary injection. The patient expressed her gratitude, and the doctor seemed pleased—though he said he would have to "consult his pillow upon it."

The next day, when Miss Seward called, the doctor took her into his study and told her he had abandoned the idea. "The construction of a proper machine is so nice an affair," said he, "the least failure in its power of acting so hazardous, the chance at last from the experiment so precarious, that I do not choose to stake my reputation upon the risk. If she die, the world will say I killed Lady Northesk, though the London and Bath physicians have pronounced her case hopeless, and sent her home to expire. They have given her a great deal too much medicine. I shall give her very little. Their system of nutritious food, their gravy jellies, and strong wines, I have already changed for milk, vegetables, and fruit. No wines ever; no meat, no strong broth, at present. . . . If this alteration of diet prove unavailing, her family and friends must lose her.''

It was not unavailing. Three weeks later Lady Northesk returned home a different woman. In time she recovered completely, and would have lived to a ripe old age if she hadn't been burnt to death by setting fire to her clothes. . . .

Now, in spite of what will appear hereafter, we must remember that Darwin was easily the greatest doctor of his day. George III heard of his fame from Lady Charlotte Finch, governess to Queen Charlotte's daughters, and said: ''Why does not Dr. Darwin come to London? He shall be my physician if he comes.'' And he repeated this over and over again in his usual manner. But apparently Darwin was quite free from vanity and ambition. He went on doing his job where circumstances had placed him. Anna Seward could never understand why he persistently ''withstood solicitations from countless families of rank and opulence to remove to London,'' and she tells us that ''the most brilliant prospects of success in the capital were opened to him . . . as a physician his renown still increased as time rolled on. . . . Patients resorted to him, more and more, from every part of the kingdom, and often from the Continent. All ranks, all orders of society, all religions leaned upon his power to ameliorate disease, and to prolong existence. The rigid and sternly pious, who had attempted to renounce his aid from a supposition that no blessing would attend the pre-scriptions of a sceptic, sacrificed, after a time, their superstitious scruples to their involuntary consciousness of his mighty skill.''

Anna was always a little worried about the doctor's '' irreligion, and encomiums on the terrible and tyrannic democracy of France,'' but she saw no reason why his shocking opinions should tell against his poetical and medical achievements. She had, of course, frequently benefited by his skill. '' To a stubborn and feverish cough,'' she confides to a friend, '' succeeded a violent inflammation in my eyes. I endured it a fortnight, every person's infallible remedy seeming to increase the malady, till, applying to Dr. Darwin, it was soon removed by his healing skill.'' All his friends have the same tale to tell. Edgeworth writes to him: '' You, my dear doctor, did perceive my disease before it was visible to vulgar sight. . . . I never took any drugs except of your prescription. . . .''

Yet, on the whole, the verdict must go against Edgeworth's assertion that the methods of his friend were not experimental and risky. '' A fool,'' said the doctor, '' is a man who never tried an experiment in his life.'' Darwin spent his life making experiments, though he was cautious enough when on dangerous ground, as we have seen in the case of Lady Northesk.

His own family was not exempt from his experiments. It struck him that the rigour of measles, like that of smallpox, could be lessened by inoculation. So he tried it on his son Robert and an infant daughter. But as the former became extremely ill, and the latter died in her first year, he did not repeat the experiment. One of the reasons for his success as a doctor is hinted at by Anna Seward:

"Extreme was his scepticism to human truth. From that cause he often disregarded the accounts his patients gave of themselves, and rather chose to collect his information by indirect inquiry, and by cross-examining them, than from their voluntary testimony. That distrust and that habit were probably favourable to his skill in discovering the origin of diseases, and thence to his pre-eminent success in effecting their cure—but they impressed his mind and tinctured his conversation with an apparent want of confidence in mankind, which was apt to wound the ingenuous and confiding spirit, whether seeking his medical assistance, or his counsel as a friend." Anna might perhaps have added: " or his reciprocation as a lover."

When Darwin commenced practice he kept accurate accounts, and the steady rise of his professional earnings during the first sixteen years of his residence in Lichfield was a solid testimony to his success. From January 1757 to January 1758 his income was £192 10s. 6d. From January 1772 to January 1773 it was £1025 3s. Multiply the latter sum by four to get its rough equivalent to-day. If he had not spent so much of his time and labour among the poorer classes, from whom he refused to take fees and to whom he usually gave medicines and food, his income might easily have been trebled. The fact that, according to his brother, he was "always seeking to do good" must have told heavily against his bank balance. . . .

Let us now open his Commonplace Book, where we may see diagrams of curious machines side by side with diagnoses of strange diseases, and observations on the wind and weather mixed up with notes on jaundice and dropsy. A glance at some of the medical entries may even reconcile us to life in the twentieth century.

1. A gentleman named Mr. Jauncey was "blooded nine times for pleurisy. He then became feeble," adds the doctor. (Not without cause, we must conclude.)

2. A certain Mrs. G. M. was afflicted with melancholia "for several weeks after parturition; nor was this the first time . . . pain about the forehead . . . causeless fears and most in the night." The doctor ordered "three double teeth which had holes in them to be extracted." The operator broke off another tooth while he was on the job and failed to get the roots out; came again the next morning and got them out. Then the doctor gave her a giant purge, "and after a stool or two she said she was perfectly well and . . . suckled her child." (The prospect of anything from a dozen to a score or so babies must have induced melancholia in most women of the eighteenth century from the moment they caught sight of the altar. Mrs. G. M. was lucky to get rid of it with her teeth.)

3. " Mr. Harrison took four draughts of foxglove, vomited a little and then purged twenty times with great debility; had next day but one a violent inflammation of the liver with much pain." (The doctor gives no indication as to whether or not he lived happpily ever after.)

4. " Mrs. Clark had her under-eyelid so turned in that the hairs were constantly covered by the eyeball. The eye had been kept thus in a painful and inflamed state for several months. I applied a slip of sticking plaster from the upper part of the ala of the nose to the temple, and put under it a hard compress about the size of a pea, which kept the cilia turned outwards in its natural place; and in a fortnight it kept there spontaneously, and became quite well. This gave me much satisfaction, as I had seen Chev. Taylor fail in effecting this by a cruel operation of cutting away a piece of skin between the eyelid and the external prominent part of the cheek-bone, and drawing together the lips of the wound with a needle and thread." (The doctor was always horrified by unnecessary cruelty. One day he went to see a vet " cut a beast for the turn or vertigo," was disgusted at the brutality of the operation and noted a gentler alternative: " Could not a covered needle be introduced into the sinus and prick the bladder? So I have heard in Paris a woman used to procure miscarriage for hire. Could not a smaller hole with a trocar and capula be used instead of this violent operation? ")

5. " Mrs. Holbeck had pain in the middle of the

breast-bone after pleurisy and inflammation, which terminated in a locked jaw. After having in vain endeavoured to inject a fluid into her mouth far enough to be swallowed, by means of a syringe introduced between two teeth which were more distant from each other than the rest, I rolled up five grains of opium into a long cylinder, introduced it into the interstice between the teeth, and pushed it forwards towards the throat by means of a thin crow-quill, and in about two hours the spasm ceased and she talked and drank as usual; but was left with great thirst and vomiting, as is usual after so large a dose of opium." (Mrs. Holbeck was lucky to get off with a vomiting, which in those days everyone had to endure, whatever the illness.)

6. "Mr. Seville had laboured several weeks with the jaundice, and taken calomel, steel, oil, etc., in vain —he had no pain, nor sickness, nor fever. I had pretty potent electric shocks passed through the body and taken out about the region of the gall bladder, and he began to mend the next day, and on continuing the electricity recovered fast." (Modern medicine could do no better.)

7. Many fashionable doctors believe nowadays that, when their patients are suffering from flea-bite or cancer or anything else, their one chance of recovery is to have all their teeth out. Dr. Darwin, though he did not go so far as his successors, seems to have paid a lot of attention to teeth and thus formulated a plan of campaign which has led to startling results. One

of his patients, Mrs. Stubs, complained that her throat was sore. He noticed that all her teeth were decayed. "I have advised her teeth to be drawn and ten or twenty electric shocks from a pint or quart phial to be passed through the sore part twice a day for a month." Then follows this terrifying phrase: "All these patients die in the common ways of treatment, whether with mercury or not." (Apparently Mrs. Stubs recovered. Then what on earth could have killed her? Perhaps she is still alive.)

8. Mrs. Parke of Newport had headaches. The doctor bled her copiously, purged her, and had a wisdom tooth extracted. The ache changed from one side of the head to the other. Another tooth was extracted. Her headaches disappeared. (Or did she say they had disappeared in order to save her teeth?)

9. Sir Charles Holt's coachman, aged forty, "seemed an habitual drinker; had the confluent smallpox to the greatest degree . . . one pock on the back of each hand about two inches diameter, and his cheeks were only one pock each. He was quite full all over. . . ." Calomel, purgings, opium, and "plaister of the emplastrum adhesium spread on linen and afterwards on London brown paper . . . renewed night and morning. He was kept airy, and rather cool, had as much small beer as he chose, and towards the eleventh day had one sixth of ale mixed with it. . . . Recovered beyond my most sanguine expectation in respect to every symptom. . . ." (Another proof that the doctor was no fanatic with regard to drink. Doubtless the small

beer kept the coachman from fretting, and gave the purgings and plaister a chance.)

10. " Mrs. —— was asthmatic and dropsical, but did not appear near her end. She took four draughts of the decoction of foxglove, as directed. . . . She vomited two or three times, and then purged twice, and died upon the close-stool." (One hesitates to comment on this case. It looks a little too much like murder.)

During those relatively short periods when the invalids of the eighteenth century were neither evacuating nor vomiting, they could always fall back on phlebotomy. Indeed one cannot sufficiently admire our ancestors for the care-free way in which the males caroused and the females committed matrimony; because anything short of absolute asceticism had such dire results.

The doctor's frequent references to ulcers and ascarides lead one to suppose they were very prevalent. He recommended the waters of " Harrow Gate " for the latter disease; while for asthma he chiefly prescribed cold and fresh air. The Commonplace Book is full of entries concerning his patients, but they are only of interest to doctors. One entry, however, must not be passed over:

" Dec. 25, 1778. I have this day seen a Mrs. Riley of Stafford, who has a diseased digestion."

No comment on the fact that he had travelled from Lichfield to Stafford on Christmas Day in order to see a stranger with a stomach-ache. Just that single sentence. . . . It tells us more about the man than volumes of testimonials from his friends.

He seldom refers to his own ailments, and he never allows them to keep him at home:

Augt. 10, 1779. Yesterday on walking about the town I felt a pain with a tension about the joint of the great toe of my right foot, which continued most part of the day. A day or two before I had felt a fullness about my stomach or liver, and a degree of sickness on eating hastily. This morning about three I waked with much pain, and tumour and redness about the joint of the toe. I bled immediately to about 10 or 12 ounces. My pulse was not much quickened nor much hard. About 4 I took calomel, gr. 6. At six this operated. At seven I was very faint and had a slight chillness and 3 or 4 more stools. At eight I put æther repeatedly on the tumid and red part ; kept it from evaporating by a piece of oiled silk. The pain became less. At nine I set out for Burton ; with difficulty got into the chaise. At eleven was easier ; went on to Aston ; at 4 or 6 p.m. was quite easy. Took a grain of opium at night ; had not return ; the swelling in two days subsided and the skin peeled off. About March 10, 1780, I had a similar fit of less violence. I only lost blood ; travelled every day, wearing a large cloth shoe, and got well in about four days, and then totally left off all spirituous potation.

On April 27, 1780, having abstained about six weeks from all spirituous potation, I had another slight attack of the gout in the joint only of the right toe (the right toe always) which continued so as not to oblige me to change my shoe, nor so as to keep me awake, for three days.

Nov. 13, 1787. After eating much salt ham and drinking near a pint of beer contrary to my custom, having many years totally abstained from spirituous drinks, I felt a debility at night, and next day had a little gout—the next more, still more on the third ; took six grains of calomel and had but one restless night.   The top of the foot and right toe swelled considerably.

One of his many contributions to the periodicals of the day contained an idea that has since blossomed out into a science. He was probably the first person to realize all the dangers of taboos and suppressions; and in his assertion that people should be encouraged to discuss their mental, moral, and physical ailments, lay the seed of psycho-analysis.

Darwin's prestige towards the end of his life was so enormous that famous physicians often wrote for his advice in cases they could not cope with. One day, towards the close of his career, he received a call from a gentleman who was in the last stages of consumption. The doctor could tell almost at once that it was a hopeless case, and was wondering how to break the news when his visitor saved him a lot of trouble by addressing him thus:

"I am come from London to consult you, as the greatest physician in the world, to hear from you if there is any hope in my case. I know that my life hangs upon a thread, but while there is life there may be hope. It is of the utmost importance for me to settle my worldly affairs immediately; therefore I trust that you will not deceive me, but tell me without hesitation your candid opinion."

Dr. Darwin felt his pulse, examined him minutely, and said he was sorry to say there was no hope.

"How long can I live?" asked the gentleman.

"Perhaps a fortnight," replied the doctor.

"Thank you, doctor, I thank you," exclaimed the

gentleman, clasping his hand; "my mind is satisfied; I now know there is no hope for me."

"But why did you come all the way from London?" asked Darwin; "why did you not consult your leading physician, Dr. Warren?"

"Alas! doctor, I am Dr. Warren," said the gentleman. He died soon afterwards. . . .

CHAPTER XI

ON THE ROAD

"To Doctor Darwin—On the Road." He once received a letter with that superscription. And that is how one usually pictures him. The greater part of his life was spent in his carriage; and the greater part of his work was written in it. His thoughts came with the jolts, and his poetry was shaken out of him.

In those days the roads were appalling; in fact they were not what we understand as roads at all. Deep and muddy ruts, sloughs, quagmires, holes two and three feet deep, boulders, sandy bottoms—these and other obstacles made travelling a tiresome and dangerous business. The dislocation of bones was a common occurrence. "A gentleman in the country," says a writer of that period, "or a citizen in London, thinks no more of visiting his relations than traversing the deserts of Nubia." In the winter many of the roads were impassable, and even at the best of times a carriage could hardly reach some of the houses the doctor had to visit. On such occasions he would get out and mount a horse, ready saddled, that used to follow his carriage without being fastened to it. This horse was called "Doctor," and lived to a great age.

People wondered how Darwin could stand the endless

fatigue of his journeys. "How strong must the corporal structure of Dr. Darwin's brain have been," exclaims Anna Seward, "which enabled him to write constantly in his chaise, from early life to his latest year!" And yet at the age of seventy he could still tell his son that five or six additional miles in the day's round made him no more tired than usual.

As the carriage swayed and jolted and pitched and lurched, the doctor's mind leapt from one subject to another with an unexampled ease and agility. There was scarcely a topic he did not touch, and nothing he touched that he did not touch up. Let us peep over his shoulder and see what he scribbles down one day as he goes from patient to patient. . . .

He has been reading a book on witches, and it appears that "these unhappy people did actually swim on the water they were plunged into." How to account for this? Simple. "In hysteric hypochondriac people, which diseases are producible by fear or anxiety, the digestion becomes impaired and the stomach and bowels become distended with air, whence Mr. Pomme found many of these patients incapable of sinking in the cold bath."

He glances at a book by Priestley, which gives him an idea. Down it goes. "There is reason to believe from some of Dr. Priestley's experiments that air which has been breathed, by being washed in water becomes fit to breathe again. Suppose a person was to put his head under a small diving bell and by such a pump as that described on the reverse page could throw a stream continually in showers about the bell, would it not sufficiently purify the air? . . . This experiment with a candle and a syphon inverted under a cock might be easily tried." (Note the sequel. On 7 November, 1928, a giant advertisement of a New Wonder Tobacco Factory appeared in the English papers. It consisted of the following announcement by the owner of the business: " I have watched this factory of my dreams become a wonderful reality. But of the thousand improvements that progress has made possible ONE installation stands out because it is the only one of its kind in the whole tobacco industry. The weather inside is controlled automatically! Whether doors or windows are open or shut; whether London is in the grip of a severe frost; or sweltering under a summer sun; or enveloped in the mugginess of a November fog—by means of a scientific apparatus the incoming air is washed with water and its humidity and tempera- ture adjusted, so that every day is a perfect day. . . .")

Water reminds the doctor of other things. " The juice of the grape, by fermentation, is the curse of the Christian world," he writes, " producing more than half of our chronical diseases; which Mahomet observed, and forbade the use of it to his disciples." And there is another deleterious item. Salt, he opines, weakens our systems; it is " the only fossil substance which the caprice of mankind has yet taken into their stomachs along with their food."

He looks out of the window and sees a dog sniffing its way along the road. " Other animals," he scribbles, " use their smell voluntarily every minute, we ours only when we detect odours and stinks; hence ours is obedient to sensation, and tears are the consequence unknown to animals but from stimulus."

This reminds him of something else: "As the sleep of animals consists in a suspension of voluntary motion, and as vegetables are likewise subject to sleep, there is reason to conclude that the various actions of opening and closing their petals and foliage may be justly ascribed to a voluntary power: for without the faculty of volition sleep would not have been necessary to them." Another point: "I was this morning surprised to observe the manifest adultery of several females of the plant Collinsonia, who had bent themselves into contact with the males of other flowers of the same plant in their vicinity, neglectful of their own." But then, for that matter, plants are "themselves animals, though of an inferior order."

He takes a novel from the pile of books at his side, reads it with little interest, and soon puts it back, making this comment: "The high-wrought scenes of elegant distress displayed in novels have been found to blunt the feelings of readers towards real objects of misery."

He comes to a village and sees a crowd round a preacher on the green. He observes the waving arms and impassioned speech of the orator and his pencil records his reflection: "Many theatric preachers among the Methodists successfully inculcate the fear of death and of hell, and live luxuriously on the folly of their hearers. The latter have so much intellectual cowardice that they dare not reason about those things which they are directed by their priests to believe."

But the sight of the preacher has given him an appetite; so, after noting that the first law of nature is " eat or be eaten," he falls to. . . .

Again he picks up Priestley's book and a further idea strikes him: " Since Dr. Priestley's discovery of the production of pure air in such abundance, it is probable in another half-century that it may be safer to travel under the ocean than over it." He puts the idea into poetry and foretells the submarine:

> Led by the Sage, Lo ! Britain's sons shall guide
> Huge sea-balloons beneath the tossing tide ;
> The diving castles, roof'd with spheric glass,
> Ribb'd with strong oak, and barr'd with bolts of brass,
> Buoy'd with pure air shall endless tracks pursue,
> And Priestley's hand the vital flood renew.

From Priestley it is an easy transition to Watt, whose improvement of the steam-engine opens up boundless possibilities, one of which he notes down: " There seems no probable method of flying conveniently but by the power of steam, or some other explosive material; which another half-century may probably discover." He enshrines the idea in verse and prophesies the aeroplane:

> Soon shall thy arm, unconquer'd Steam ! afar
> Drag the small barge, or drive the rapid car ;
> Or on wide-waving wings expanded bear
> The flying-chariot through the fields of air.
> Fair crews triumphant, leaning from above,
> Shall wave their fluttering kerchiefs as they move ;
> Or warrior-bands alarm the gaping crowd,
> And armies shrink beneath the shadowy cloud.

This brings him to the absurd restriction of human faculty and ability: "Nature may seem to have been niggardly to mankind in bestowing upon them so few senses; since a sense to have perceived electricity, and another to have perceived magnetism, might have been of great service to them many ages before these fluids were discovered by accidental experiment; but it is possible an increased number of senses might have incommoded us by adding to the size of our bodies."

Nevertheless man has it in him to improve himself out of all recognition. "The thinking few in all ages," he jots down, "have complained of the brevity of life, lamenting that mankind are not allowed time sufficient to cultivate science, or to improve their intellect." Anticipating Mr. Bernard Shaw, he can find no adequate reason why people should die at all except from habit. He goes into the matter at considerable length, catalogues a number of "means of preventing old age," and suggests that it might "have been easier for nature to have continued her animals and vegetables for ever in their mature state, than perpetually by a complicated apparatus to have produced new ones, and suffer the old ones to perish."

This opens up a new line of thought. Far more people kill themselves off by disease than die of old age; and not only themselves but their descendants. Thus it becomes necessary to breed only from the healthy; and instantly the science of Eugenics, as worked out by his grandson, Francis Galton, is conceived by the doctor: "The art to improve the sexual progeny of either vegetables or animals must consist in choosing the most perfect of both sexes, that is the most beautiful in respect to the body, and the most ingenious in respect to the mind; but where one sex is given, whether male or female, to improve a progeny from that person may consist in choosing a partner of a contrary temperament. As many families become gradually extinct by hereditary diseases, as by scrofula, consumption, epilepsy, mania, it is often hazardous to marry an heiress, as she is not unfrequently the last of a diseased family.''

The mention of mania turns his mind into other channels. Lunatics in his day were brutally ill-treated; he had done his best to explain the absurdity and inhumanity of '' flogging them back to their senses.'' Better let them run loose in the world than deliver them over to such barbarity. So his busy pencil travels on: '' No lunatic should be restrained unless he be dangerous. Confinement retards rather than promotes their cure, which is forwarded by change of ideas, etc.'' He then remarks that mistaken ideas do not by themselves justify confinement, adding: '' If everyone who possesses mistaken ideas, or who puts false estimates on things, was liable to confinement, I know not who of my readers might not tremble at the sight of a madhouse.'' (For all this, of course, is going into a book one fine day.)

From the horrors of the lunatic asylum it is a short step to the horrors of the prison, and he writes a lengthy eulogium of Howard, the great prison reformer, which contains this couplet:

> He treads inemulous of fame or wealth,
> Profuse of toil, and prodigal of health.

And from that to the horror of horrors, which haunts him continually—" the detestable traffic in human creatures," known as the slave-trade. When he " sees red " he usually turns to verse:

Heavens ! on my sight what sanguine colours blaze !
Spain's deathless shame ! the crime of modern days !
When Avarice, shrouded in Religion's robe,
Sail'd to the West, and slaughtered half the globe ;
While Superstition, stalking by his side,
Mock'd the loud groans, and lap'd the bloody tide ;
For sacred truths announced her frenzied dreams,
And turn'd to night the sun's meridian beams.—
Hear, oh, Britannia ! potent Queen of isles,
On whom fair Art, and meek Religion smiles,
Now Afric's coasts thy craftier sons invade
With murder, rapine, theft,—and call it Trade !
——The Slave, in chains, on supplicating knee,
Spreads his wide arms, and lifts his eyes to Thee ;
With hunger pale, with wounds and toil oppress'd,
" Are we not Brethren ? " sorrow choaks the rest ;
——Air ! bear to heaven upon thy azure flood
Their innocent cries !—Earth ! cover not their blood !

Then, coming down to brass tacks, he seizes a piece of note-paper and dashes off a letter to Wedgwood:

I have just heard that there are muzzles or gags made at Birmingham for the slaves in our islands. If this be true, and such an instrument could be exhibited by a speaker in the House of Commons, it might have a great effect. Could not one of their long whips or wire tails be also procured and exhibited ? But an instrument of torture of our own manufacture would have a greater effect, I daresay.

His muse, however, will not be satisfied. He has something else to tell the world:

Hark ! heard ye not that piercing cry,
   Which shook the waves, and rent the sky !—
E'en now, e'en now, on yonder Western shores
Weeps pale Despair, and writhing Anguish roars :
E'en now in Afric's groves with hideous yell
Fierce Slavery stalks, and slips the dogs of hell ;
From vale to vale the gathering cries rebound,
And sable nations tremble at the sound !—
—Ye Bands of Senators ! whose suffrage sways
Britannia's realms, whom either Ind obeys ;
Who right the injured, and reward the brave,
Stretch your strong arm, for ye have power to save !
   The close recesses of the heart within,
Stern Conscience sits, the arbiter of Sin ;
With still small voice the plots of Guilt alarms,
Lights his dark mind, his lifted hand disarms ;
But, wrap'd in night with terrors all his own,
He speaks in thunder, when the deed is done.
Hear him, ye Senates ! hear this truth sublime,
"HE, WHO ALLOWS OPPRESSION, SHARES THE CRIME."

No radiant pearl, which crested Fortune wears,
No gem, that twinkling hangs from Beauty's ears,
Not the bright stars, which night's blue arch adorn,
Nor vernal suns, that gild the rising morn,
Shine with such lustre as the tear, that breaks
For others' woe down Virtue's manly cheeks.

The thoughts engendered by the slavery question are
disturbed by a professional call, and when he returns to
his chaise he is thinking of something else. He has
just seen a woman suckling her child, and it occurs to
him that " our ideas of beauty are acquired in early
infancy from the curved lines of a female's bosom.
. . . Hence at our maturer years, when any object of

vision is presented to us, which by its waving or spiral lines bears any similitude to the form of the female bosom, whether it be found in a landscape with soft gradations of rising and descending surface, or in the forms of some antique vases, or in other works of the pencil or the chisel, we feel a general glow of delight, which seems to influence all our senses; and if the object be not too large" (the doctor has just remembered Ben Nevis in time) "we experience an attraction to embrace it with our arms and to salute it with our lips, as we did in our early infancy the bosom of our mother."

And there is another sensation we get from the same source. "The origin of the smile," remarks the doctor, "has generally been ascribed to inexplicable instinct, but may be deduced from our early associations of actions and ideas. In the act of sucking, the lips of the infant are closed round the nipple of its mother, till it has filled its stomach, and the pleasure of digesting this grateful food succeeds; then the sphincter of the mouth, fatigued by the continued action of sucking, is relaxed; and the antagonist muscles of the face gently acting, produce the smile of pleasure, which is thus during our lives associated with gentle pleasure."

The reverse of that beauty and that pleasure presents itself to him as his carriage bumps its way past a foul well and a churchyard. He looks a century or so ahead, and this is what we read:

" The sewage from towns and villages, which is now buried in wells or thrown into rivers, should be removed for the purpose of agriculture; and thus the purity and healthiness of the towns may contribute to the thriftiness and wealth of the surrounding country." Also " there should be no burial places in churches or church-yards, where the monuments of departed sinners shoulder God's altar, pollute his holy places with dead men's bones, and produce by putrid exhalations contagious diseases among those who frequent his worship; but proper burial-grounds should be consecrated out of towns."

This begets a further thought. Perhaps dirt produces germs too minute to be seen by the naked eye. " I hope," he writes, " that microscopic researches may again excite the attention of philosophers, as unforeseen advantages may probably be derived from them like the discovery of a new world." (He was right. Such researches discovered a new world more than half a century after he wrote the words, and resulted in Lord Lister's antiseptic treatment of wounds, which revolutionized surgery.)

There is a copy of *Don Quixote* among the books by his side. He opens it at a chance page and reads the Knight's denunciation of gunpowder, which " levels the strong with the weak." The doctor pooh-poohs the notion and makes this comment: " The discovery of gunpowder has been of public utility by weakening the tyranny of the few over the many."

The copy of *Don Quixote* is an old edition with the quaint spelling of the previous century. This opens up a new line of investigation. He writes a multitude of notes on the theory and structure of language, a lengthy analysis of articulate sounds, and concludes: " The alphabet is yet in a very imperfect state; perhaps seventeen letters could express all the simple sounds in the European languages. . . . The active and ingenious of all nations should attend to those sciences which better the condition of human nature." (The active and ingenious did nothing in the matter for over a century, but they are just beginning to wake up to its importance.)

From phonetics and etymology he slips easily into a disquisition on moss-drainage and anemology, and after going carefully into the questions of agriculture and gardening, and supplying by diagram an improved drill plough, he reaches one of his favourite topics—the kinship of all nature.

He has just been looking through Plato, and begins his reflections thus: " The famous sentence of Socrates, ' Know thyself' . . . however wise it may be, seems to be rather of a selfish nature, and the author of it might have added ' Know also other people.' But the sacred maxims of the author of Christianity, ' Do as you would be done by,' and ' Love your neighbour as yourself,' include all our duties of benevolence and morality; and, if sincerely obeyed by all nations, would a thousandfold multiply the present happiness of mankind." (What would Mrs. " Skim " have thought if she could have peeped with us over his shoulder and seen him write that?)

The doctor's sense of kinship with all nature, from fish to fossils, makes him unconsciously funny, as when he refers to " the lone truffle "; though perhaps there is a glint of merriment in his eye as he pens: " Hence when a monarch or a mushroom dies."

But this feeling of a universal relationship never leaves him. Though he can write:

> Air, earth, and ocean, to astonish'd day
> One scene of blood, one mighty tomb display !
> From Hunger's arm the shafts of Death are hurl'd,
> And one great Slaughter-house the warring world !

he still feels that something can be done about it. Nor does this affect his argument that men, beasts, and vegetables are subject to the same life-processes:

> Thus the tall Oak, the giant of the wood,
> Which bears Britannia's thunders on the flood ;
> The Whale, unmeasured monster of the main,
> The lordly Lion, monarch of the plain,
> The Eagle soaring in the realms of air,
> Whose eyes undazzled drinks the solar glare,
> Imperious man, who rules the bestial crowd,
> Of language, reason, and reflection proud,
> With brow erect who scorns this earthy sod,
> And styles himself the image of his God ;
> Arose from rudiments of form and sense,
> An embryon point, or microscopic ens !

And he observes: " The great Creator of all things has infinitely diversified the works of his hands, but has at the same time stamped a certain similitude on the features of nature, that demonstrates to us that *the whole is one family of one parent*."

It follows that man has nothing much to make a song about:

> Stoop, selfish Pride ! survey thy kindred forms,
> Thy brother Emmets, and thy sister Worms!

But no need to despair on that account. "Perhaps all the productions of nature are in their progress to greater perfection!—an idea countenanced by modern discoveries and deductions concerning the progressive formation of the solid parts of the terraqueous globe, and consonant to the dignity of the Creator of all things. . . . For there is more dignity in our idea of the supreme Author of all things when we conceive him to be the cause of causes than the cause simply of the events, which we see; if there can be any difference in infinity of power!"

As he writes the words the evening is coming on and he observes the curious fact that "the twilight of the evenings is lighter than that of the mornings at the same distance from noon." There are reasons for this and he jots them down. His carriage is now ascending a hill from a misty valley, and he sees "a beautiful coloured halo round the moon . . . which ceased to be visible as soon as I emerged from the mist." This recalls a similar experience: "I well remember admiring with other spectators the shadow of the three spires of the cathedral church of Lichfield, the moon rising behind it, apparently broken off, and lying distinctly over our heads as if horizontally on the surface of the mist, which arose about as high as the roof of the church." More reasons noted. He then goes into the question of ocular delusions, explains the possible origins of the *ignis fatuus* or jack o' lantern, and confesses: "I have travelled much in the night, in all seasons of the year, and over all kinds of soil, but never saw one of these will o' wisps."

He calls on a patient who is dying. He has seen many deaths in his time, but he never becomes quite hardened to it. He turns to philosophy: " When we reflect on the perpetual destruction of organic life, we should also recollect that it is perpetually renewed in other forms by the same materials, and thus the sum-total of the happiness of the world continues undiminished; and that a philosopher may thus smile again on turning his eyes from the coffins of nature to her cradles."

Everywhere he sees evidence of design, of mind and meaning in the universe—in the protective stings and thorns of nettles and shrubs, in the defensive poisons of certain plants, in the colours of flowers, insects, birds, and beasts. " All vegetables and animals now existing," he cries, " were originally derived from the smallest microscopic ones, formed by spontaneous vitality; and they have by innumerable reproductions, during innumerable centuries of time, gradually acquired the size, strength, and excellence of form and faculties which they now possess. Such amazing powers were originally impressed on matter and spirit by the great Parent of Parents! Cause of Causes! Ens Entium!" A philosopher has but to catch " a glimpse of the general economy of nature; and, like the mariner cast upon an unknown shore, who rejoiced when he saw the print of a human foot upon the land, he will cry out with rapture, ' A God Dwells Here!'"

The doctor leaves his last patient, and as his carriage clatters home through the deepening gloom, he commits his creed to paper, giving a new faith to humanity:

" Cause and effect may be considered as the progression, or successive motions, of the parts of the great system of Nature. The state of things at this moment is the effect of the state of things which existed in the preceding moment, and the cause of the state of things which shall exist in the next moment. . . .

" This perpetual chain of causes and effects, whose first link is riveted to the throne of God, divides itself into innumerable diverging branches, which, like the nerves arising from the brain, permeate the most minute and most remote extremities of the system, diffusing motion and sensation to the whole. As every cause is superior in power to the effect which it has produced, so our idea of the power of the Almighty Creator becomes more elevated and sublime, as we trace the operations of nature from cause to cause, climbing up the links of these chains of being, till we ascend to the Great Source of all things.

" Hence the modern discoveries in chemistry and in geology, by having traced the causes of the combinations of bodies to remoter origins, as well as those in astronomy, which dignify the present age, contribute to enlarge and amplify our ideas of the power of the Great First Cause. And had those ancient philosophers, who contended that the world was formed from atoms, ascribed their combinations to certain immutable properties received from the hand of the Creator, such as general gravitation, chemical affinity, or animal appetency, instead of ascribing them to a blind chance; the doctrine of atoms, as constituting or composing the material world by the variety of their combinations, so far from leading the mind to atheism, would strengthen the demonstration of the existence of a Deity, as the first cause of all things; because the analogy resulting from our perpetual experience of cause and effect would have thus been exemplified through universal nature.

" 'The heavens declare the glory of God, and the firmament showeth his handiwork! . . . Manifold are thy works, O Lord! in wisdom hast thou made them all.' "

CHAPTER XII

DERBY AND DEATH

So now, where Derwent rolls his dusky floods,
Through vaulted mountains, and a night of woods. . . .

HIS removal to Derby prevented the doctor from attending most of the Lunar meetings. He felt this keenly, but his domestic happiness more than made up for the loss. His labours, however, did not decrease. He had no use for what Macaulay called "torpid repose." Doctoring still occupied his days and poetry still kept his pencil busy as he went on his rounds.

In anticipation of a smallpox epidemic among the poor of Derby, he drew up a plan for a dispensary, in which there appears this eminently Darwinian clause: "That the names of the patients and their respective places of residence, together with their recovery, relief, or the contrary, shall be published annually; that the subscribers may judge of the utility of the establishment, and in consequence either continue or withdraw their subscriptions." No hocus-pocus about that! He proposed that the medical men of the town should give their attendance gratuitously, and that, in order to disarm opposition, the patients should take their prescriptions in due order to all the druggists in the town.

His common sense as a doctor was never-failing. Though convinced of the harmful effects of alcohol on the human constitution, he could yet say: "In the chronic debility brought on by drinking spirituous or fermented liquors . . . I have directed several patients to omit one-fourth part of the quantity of vinous spirit they have been lately accustomed to, and if in a fortnight their appetite increases, they are advised to omit another fourth part; but if they perceive that their digestion becomes impaired on the want of this quantity of spirituous potation, I advise them to continue as they are, and rather bear those ills they have than risk the encounter of greater."

In April 1784 he was elected an honorary member of the Literary and Philosophical Society of Manchester; and in July of the same year he founded the Philosophical Society of Derby, which was amalgamated with the Derby Town and County Museum in 1858. The first meeting of the latter took place at his own house, and in the course of his inaugural address, still preserved in his own handwriting, we read the following:

" As we are fashioned and constituted by the niggard hand of Nature with such imperfect and contracted faculties, with so few and such imperfect senses; while the bodies which surround us are indued with infinite variety of properties; with attractions, repulsions, gravitations, exhalations, polarities, minuteness, irresistance, &c., which are not cognizable by our dull organs of sense, or not adapted to them; what are we to do? Shall we sit down contented with ignorance, and after we have procured our food, sleep away our time like the inhabitants of the woods and pastures? No, certainly!—since there is another way by which we may indirectly become acquainted with those properties of bodies which escape our senses; and that is *by observing and registering their effects upon each other.* This is the tree of knowledge, whose fruit forbidden to the brute creation has been plucked by the daring hand of *experimental philosophy.* . . . I hope at some distant time, perhaps not very distant, by our own publications we may add something to the common heap of knowledge; which I prophesy will never cease to accumulate so long as the human footstep is seen upon the earth.''

Ideas continued to pour from him in such abundance that whenever people talked of him they would laugh and shake their heads—the implication being that he was a privileged jester, not quite sound in the upper story. Even Coleridge, who ought to have known better, used the expression '' Darwinizing '' as synonymous for talking crazily. It was all very well for him to say that '' animals subsist on vegetables; they take the matter so far prepared and have organs to prepare it further for the purposes of higher animation and greater sensibility ''; but it sounded silly when he went on: '' For how could a man or quadruped have carried on his head or back a forest of leaves, or have had long branching lacteal or absorbent vessels terminating in the earth?'' The eighteenth century was not prepared for humour in philosophy.

He paid several visits to London during these years, and in 1787 was made a member of the Medical Society there; but he only went to please his wife, always preferring his home life to the gaieties of the capital. He seems at this period to have been extraordinarily happy. He and his wife were devoted to one another, and all the children of his second marriage cherished in after-life the happiest memories of their youth. The doctor shared in their fun and festivities, invented all sorts of things to amuse them, and wrote nonsense-rhymes for their edification. Driving out of Derby one day with two of his boys, he pointed to a sign over an inn:

> This gate hangs well, and hinders none :
> Refresh and pay and travel on.

Which, to the huge delight of the youngsters, he parodied thus:

> This gate hangs ill, and hinders all :
> Pray travel on and do not call.

A gentleman who had clearly not profited by the doctor's advice passed them on the road, and the boys enjoyed another dose of their parent's dry muse:

> O mortal man that liv'st by bread !
> What makes thy nose to look so red ?
> 'Tis Burton Ale, so strong and stale,
> That keeps my nose from growing pale.

His daughters were always pestering him to write verses on this, that, or the other thing, and he usually managed to give them what they wanted. For example:

> Simon did vow, nay he did swear,
> He'd dance with none but who were fair.
> Suppose we women should dispense
> Our hands to none but men of sense ?
> Suppose !—well, madam, and what then ?
> Why, sir, you'd never dance again !

In 1789 Darwin published the second part of *The Botanic Garden*, which was followed by the first part in 1791. The poem was received with a chorus of praise, which, according to Miss Seward, showed such "taste and discrimination" on the part of the "hireling critics" that she felt sure he had "procured some ingenious friend or friends to fabricate the various reviews which have appeared in the public prints."

Though he had commenced writing *The Botanic Garden* when he was forty-six, he did not publish it till he was fifty-eight, because he thought it might adversely affect his practice as a doctor if he appeared before the world as a poet. In this respect he was warned by the example of Akenside, whose medical practice had suffered from his poetic fame.

But it was not only the critics who applauded the poem. Perhaps no other work in our literature had been received with such general approval by people who were not wont to lose their heads. Anna Seward's praise may not carry much weight nowadays, but she was an honest woman who had spent her life with the poets. She called Darwin "our English Ovid," "the Claude, the Salvator, and the Titian of verse." Wedgwood was enchanted, and spoke of his friend as "the powerful magician who can work wonders, who can liquefy the granite and still harder flint into the softest poetic numbers, and with the breath of his mouth waft their varied productions to the most distant ages."

Edgeworth wrote: "To have my name in a note in your work is to have it immortal. . . . I read the description of the 'Ballet of Medea' to my sisters, and to eight or ten of my own family. It seized such hold of my imagination that my blood thrilled back through my veins, and my hair broke the cementing of the friseur, to gain the attitude of horror. The ghost in *Hamlet*, by the by, only raised the unconstrained locks of an ill-combed Dane. To force nature through the obstructions of art is quite another thing. . . . Whilst I sleep, or curse, over many other descriptive poems, I shout applause when I hear yours." Edgeworth also said *The Botanic Garden* had " silenced for ever the complaint of poets who lament that Homer, Milton, Shakespeare, and a few classics had left nothing new to describe"; and he predicted that " in future times some critic will arise who shall re-discover *The Botanic Garden* and build his fame upon this discovery. . . . It will shine out again the admiration of posterity. . . ." Who knows?

Watt called him " Darwin of the silver song," and Priestley, Galton, and the rest of the " Lunatics" were unanimous in their praise. James Keir added his voice to the chorus: " I am confirmed in the opinion I always had that you would have been the first poet of the kingdom if you had not suppressed your talent. . . . The number of beautiful passages are not to be noticed, for they are without number. . . . Immortality will be your sure reward. . . . Mrs. Keir desires to join in best compliments to Mrs. Darwin and yourself. I have had the pleasure of making her forget a violent toothache by reading part of your poem to her." Could poetry do more?

Horace Walpole became a slavish admirer. " Dr.

Darwin," he said, "has destroyed my admiration for any poetry but his own," and he constantly referred to Erasmus as "the sublime, the divine." When the first part was published, he wrote to a friend: "*The Triumph of Flora*, beginning at the fifty-ninth line, is most beautifully and enchantingly imagined; and the twelve verses that by miracle describe and comprehend the creation of the universe out of chaos, are in my opinion the most sublime in any author, or in any of the few languages with which I am acquainted. There are a thousand other verses most charming, or indeed all are so, crowded with most poetic imagery, gorgeous epithets and style"—and yet he didn't like the first part as much as the second![1]

These are the lines that Walpole praised so highly:

" Let there be Light ! " proclaim'd the Almighty Lord,
Astonish'd Chaos heard the potent word ;—
Through all his realms the kindling Ether runs,
And the mass starts into a million suns ;
Earths round each sun with quick explosions burst,
And second planets issue from the first ;
Bend, as they journey with projectile force,
In bright ellipses their reluctant course ;
Orbs wheel in orbs, round centres centres roll,
And form, self-balanced, one revolving Whole.
Onward they move amid their bright abode,
Space without bound, the Bosom of their God !

Perhaps the most surprising tribute came from William Cowper, whose poetry, by the way, did not

[1] Of the second part, he wrote : " I can read this over and over again for ever . . . all, all, all is the most lovely poetry." And again : " Dr. Darwin alone can exceed his predecessors."

appeal to Darwin. Writing on behalf of himself and
Hayley, Cowper eulogized the author of *The Botanic
Garden* in this manner:

> Two Poets (poets by report
>   Not oft so well agree),
> Sweet Harmonist of Flora's court !
>   Conspire to honour Thee.
>
> They best can judge a poet's worth,
>   Who oft themselves have known
> The pangs of a poetic birth
>   By labours of their own.
>
> The verse that kindles meets a fire,
>   A kindred fire in them,
> The numbers live, that they admire,
>   And die, that they condemn.
>
> We, therefore, pleas'd, extol thy song,
>   Though various, yet complete,
> Rich in embellishment, as strong,
>   And learn'd, as it is sweet.
>
> No envy mingles with our praise,
>   Though could our hearts repine
> At any poet's happier lays,
>   They would, they must, at thine.
>
> But we in mutual bondage knit
>   Of Friendship's closest tie,
> Can gaze on even Darwin's wit
>   With an unjaundic'd eye ;
>
> And deem the Bard, whoe'er he be,
>   And howsoever known,
> Who would not twine a wreath for Thee,
>   Unworthy of his own.

Anna Seward was very angry with Darwin for having taken some lines she wrote [1] and printed them at the beginning of his poem without acknowledging her authorship. When taxed on the subject he said: "It was a compliment I felt bound to pay her." But this may only prove that he acted up to his axioms. "The doctor was accustomed to remark," says Anna, "that whenever a strange step had been taken, if in any way obnoxious to censure, the alleged reason was scarcely ever the real motive." He had previously sent her lines to a magazine, where they were published under her name, and he probably did not realize she attached much importance to them. He had not quarrelled with her when she failed to distinguish his lines in her *Ode to Captain Cook*; and as he had altered quite a number of her lines when they appeared in *The Botanic Garden*, he was justified in thinking she would have been very angry indeed if he had attributed them to her in that condition. The subject need not detain us, though it kept Anna's pen fairly busy in correspondence with everyone except the unwitting culprit for some time. [2]

The Botanic Garden was parodied in Canning's paper *The Anti-Jacobin* under the title *The Loves of the Triangles*. The Canning crowd hated Darwin for his views on the French Revolution, and this was their revenge. The parody had a great success, and Anna wrote to a friend: "If Dr. Darwin had been

[1] *Vide* Chapter IX, pp. 159-60.
[2] "After all," said Sir Walter Scott in a letter to Maria Edgeworth, "I do not think the verses very much worth struggling about."

a fair and generous decider on the literary claims of others . . . I should painfully sympathize with the mortification he is likely to feel. . . . For this loss of present universal homage, I question if Dr. D.'s mind is strong enough to feel recompense in his inevitable conviction that his poetic and his philosophic writings possess the germs of a vitality which will be coeval with the existence of the English language." The explanation of this sympathetic passage is simply that Erasmus had not appraised Anna's poetry at its right value.

But "Dr. D.'s" mind was not quite so weak as she imagined. Edgeworth tells us that when he spoke in praise of the parody to Darwin, "he appeared to think as I did of its wit, ingenuity, and poetic merit." As for Anna's constant assertions that the doctor was jealous of other people's reputations and had a high opinion of his own merits, a letter he wrote to his son in 1788 hardly bears them out: "I am printing *The Loves of the Plants*, which I shall not put my name to, though it will be known to many. But the addition of my name would seem as if I thought it a work of consequence."

Already, we have seen, in his dealings with Wedgwood over the windmill, how little disposed he was to push forward his own experiments whenever he felt they could be bettered. But we must dispose of Anna's accusations once and for all. She is quite honest enough, in a general way, to be worth the attention. Long before Watt had joined hands with Boulton, the doctor had been experimenting with a "locomotive steam engine." He wrote to Boulton, giving him full particulars of his "fiery chariot," and asking him to become a partner in the concern. Boulton thought his ideas a bit crude, and the matter was dropped. Later, when Watt joined him and they produced their first model together, Boulton received this letter from Darwin: "Your model of a steam-engine, I am told, has gained so much approbation in London that I cannot but congratulate you on the mechanical fame you have acquired by it, which, assure yourself, is as great a pleasure to me as it could possibly be to yourself."

So much for Anna. But we need not love her any the less. . . .

The success of *The Botanic Garden* was great. It went into several editions, and Darwin received a thousand guineas, in advance, for the part which was published last. His other works were also successful. They were all the result of many years' note-making and meditation, chiefly in his carriage.

Zoonomia came out in 1794. He had intended it for publication after his death, but the unassailable position he had now reached in his profession made such discretion no longer necessary. He referred to it as far back as 1775 in a letter to a friend, J. Cradock. Tha gentleman had sent him a copy of his *Village Memoirs*. Darwin, in acknowledgment, said:

What shall I send you in return? I who have for twenty years neglected the Muses, and cultivated medicine alone with all my industry? Medical Dissertations I have several finished for the press, but dare not publish them, well knowing the reception a living writer in medicine is sure to meet with from those who wish to raise their own reputation on the ruin of their antagonists. Faults may be found or invented ; or at least ridicule may cast blots on a book were it written with a pen from the wings of the angel Gabriel. I lately interceded with a Derbyshire lady to desist from lopping a grove of trees, which has occasioned me, since you saw me (I suppose from inspiration, or rather infection I might catch from you), to try again the long neglected art of verse-making, which I shall inclose to amuse you, promising, at the same time, never to write another verse as long as I live, but to apply my time to finishing a work on some branches of medicine, which I intend for a posthumous publication. . . .

Two years before it was published, Darwin wrote to his son Robert:

I am studying my *Zoonomia* which I *think* I shall publish, in hopes of selling it, as I am now too old and hardened to fear a little abuse. Every John Hunter must expect a Jesse Foot to pursue him, as a fly bites a horse.

Zoonomia, or the Laws of Organic Life, was translated into German, French, and Italian, and, in the words of Charles Darwin, "was honoured by the Pope by being placed in the Index Expurgatorius." It contains a mass of information on a hundred different subjects, and the theories contained in it were regarded as ludicrously extravagant until Samuel Butler came along and gave Darwin his due. The doctor himself had foreseen the line of attack on all his theoretical work, and had explained that "extravagant theories, in those parts of philosophy where our knowledge is yet imperfect, are not without their use; as they encourage the execution of laborious experiments, or the investigation of ingenious deductions to confirm or refute them. And since natural objects are allied to each other by many affinities, every kind of theoretic distribution of them adds to our knowledge by developing some of their analogies."

The book is, of course, chiefly medical, but it contains, among other things, the first complete view of evolution. It was he, and not his grandson Charles, who (to quote Dr. Dowson) was "the first to give a series of plausible reasons, and the best that have yet been advanced, for believing the Origin of Species by transmutation possible." Indeed, the conclusions reached as a result of his grandson's theories would have horrified him; and it is his conception of evolution that has survived, not that of Charles.

Phytologia, or the Philosophy of Agriculture and Gardening, was published in 1800. That, too, is prolific of theories, many of which are now regarded as truisms. The subjects range from flower-buds to bone-dust, and from phosphorus to ploughs.

Darwin's only other work of importance was *The Temple of Nature, or the Origin of Society*, a poem with philosophical notes, which was not published till 1803, a year after his death. . . .

Towards the end of 1789 Darwin lost his strange friend, Thomas Day. It is difficult to see what these two could have had in common, except a love of philosophy. Perhaps Day chiefly appealed to Darwin as a curious and entertaining specimen of humanity, though his practical philanthropy must also have gained the doctor's esteem. Whatever the attraction, they thought very highly of one another, and Darwin was the first person approached by Keir for details of their friend's life. The doctor told Keir that he would have to describe the Sabrina episode. Keir demurred: "What you say relating to the propriety of mentioning Mr. Day's experiment of education as being characteristic is unquestionably just, but how to execute?" Darwin apparently suggested a method which couldn't hurt the feelings of anyone concerned. Keir replied: " What you propose is too well known *not to be the accurate state*, and it could be easily contradicted, and thus the credit of the whole history brought into question." It is to be feared the doctor was in favour of tampering with history, which bears out several of Mrs. "Skim's" strictures on his character. One can almost hear him saying, " As all written history is a lie, let us make a good lie of it." Anyhow, Keir took his advice about mentioning Day's experiment, but gave a very diluted version of the story. This made Edgeworth a little peevish. "In Mr. K.'s letters to me, about Mr. Day's life," he complained to the doctor, " he spoke of my mentioning Sabrina as impossible. I now find he has changed his opinion. What can the life of a private man consist of, but of private circumstances? The *author* appears best in his works."   .

Darwin kept up an energetic correspondence with all his friends after he had removed to Derby. Mechanical experiments still occupied much of his time. He constructed a " steam wheel," and asked Wedgwood if he would care to share in its expenses and profits. Wedgwood declined on account of his age and infirmities, though he was hardly older than Darwin. An electrical machine was the next thing to exercise his brain, and this was followed by lamps. Wedgwood was interested in the lamps, and helped him; but as the doctor only found time for them during the long winter nights, the experiments extended over four years.

The Wedgwood and Darwin families were constantly exchanging visits. Miss Wedgwood, who was a great favourite with her future father-in-law, used to give him lessons in music when she came to stay at Derby. Once she brought a specimen of Josiah's work, but "Your medallion I have not yet seen," wrote the doctor to the potter; "it is covered over with so many strata of caps and ruffles, and Miss Wedgwood is whirled off to a card-party—seen and vanished like a shooting star."

Whenever the Wedgwoods travelled to London, they were expected to stay at Derby *en route*. The doctor heard of one projected trip and promptly forestalled it:

Mrs. Darwin says your whole family are going to town in a body, like a caravan going to Mecca ; and we therefore hope you will make Derby a resting-place, and recruit yourselves and your camels for a few days, after having travelled over the burning sands of Cheadle and Uttoxeter.

Wedgwood was always sending gifts to his Derby friends. One specially large consignment drew this from the doctor:

Mrs. Darwin has commissioned me to write to thank you for the very excellent Bath you have been so kind as to send her. But what was the astonishment of the family when on striking it there was heard a rattling of armour within ! Some of us began to think it like the Trojan horse, & fear'd it might contain armed warriors ; others that like Pandora's box, it might contain many evils at the top and hope at the bottom. These fears ceased on recollecting who was the kind donor, & that presents from a friend were not to be suspected like those of an enemy. So out came the straw, and with it the bowels of the pestiferous animal, beyond any power of numbering or naming, for each individual of which I am commanded to thank you over & over, & to add all our kindest compliments to you and yours.

In 1787 Wedgwood had a nervous breakdown; but with Darwin's help he was soon well again, and busy making his wonderful copy of the Barberini vase, which was lent him for that purpose by the Duke of Portland, who had just bought it for £1029. By October 1789, after scrapping several defective attempts, he had made his first perfect copy, and sent it at once to Dr. Darwin, with injunctions not to show it to a soul outside his own family. But that was asking too much of the doctor, who wrote:

I have disobeyed you, and shown your vase to two or three, but they were philosophers, not cognoscenti. How can I possess a jewel, and not communicate the pleasure to a few Derby philosophers ?

The friends met sometimes at Buxton, where Wedgwood, on the doctor's advice, now spent a little time every spring, summer, and autumn, for the sake of his health. Here Darwin usually joined him for a day or two, and they renewed their old scientific discussions, the hours passing all too quickly. Wedgwood's sobriety of judgment was a good foil to the daring flights of Darwin's keen and previsional intellect.

In 1794 Wedgwood was again ill. Ever since the amputation he had suffered pain in what Darwin called his " no leg," and now there were other troubles. He experienced shortness of breath, which the doctor ascribed " to the distant approach of age and not to asthma—you know how unwilling we all are to grow old." Then his face began to swell, and the local surgeon discovered early symptoms of mortification. He grew worse, his throat became inflamed, and his weakness increased. Dr. Darwin hastened over from Derby and watched sedulously by his bedside. But nothing could save him. He suffered greatly at first; then he became insensible, and in that condition he died on 3 January, 1795. " The death of Mr. Wedgwood grieves me very much," wrote Darwin to Edgeworth; " he is a public as well as a private loss. We all grow old but you! When I think of dying, it is always without pain or fear."

Edgeworth had now settled in Ireland, where he was experimenting with railways, telegraphy, bog-drainage, and politics. Needless to say, the doctor had a scheme for bog-drainage, which Edgeworth carried through with success. He was about to marry his fourth wife, and had already lost count of his children. In spite of the doctor's warning that he would be " torn to pieces by the teeth and fangs of the parliamentary leaders," he entered the Irish Parliament, and even had the temerity to quote the doctor's opinions in several debates. In 1791 he stayed with his friend at Derby.

They had tremendous discussions on mechanics and literature, during which Darwin asked him to "breathe the breath of life into the brazen lungs of a clock," laughed heartily when Edgeworth confessed to a fondness for *The Arabian Nights*, and advised him and his daughter Maria to write books on education. They took his advice.

Back again in Ireland, Edgeworth wrote a long letter about his telegraphic experiments, and after three months got this answer from the doctor:

I beg your pardon for not immediately answering your last favor, which was owing to the great influence the evil demon has at present in all affairs on this earth. That is, I lost your letter, and have in vain looked over some scores of papers, and cannot find it. Secondly, having lost your letter, I daily hoped to find it again—without success. . . .

I kept this letter three or four days, to send you a legal receipt, and now I don't know how to send you one. Mr. Burns, the Quaker, once let me a lease, which began with—" Friend Darwin, honest men need no lawyer, I hereby let you a lease," &c. So I send you my receipt, as follows . . . without technical form.

Adieu ; your sincere and affectionate friend, E. DARWIN.

A picture of the doctor was sent to Edgeworth in 1798, but didn't please him: " It does not give an idea of any faculty of your mind, except ingenuity;—there is a cloud over your brow, and a compression of the lips, that hide your benevolence and good humour. . . . I observe with pleasure, mixed with pride, the rapid growth of your fame. . . ."

A year later Edgeworth took his family over to England, and they all went to stay with the Darwins.

Maria Edgeworth was delighted with the doctor, whom she called "the common friend of genius and of goodness, which he had the happy talent of discovering, attracting, and attaching." He also attracted other types of people, of whom, it is possible, Miss Edgeworth might not have approved. Sir Brooke Boothby, a dissipated country gentleman, once declared (doubtless between hiccups): "Darwin was one of the best men I have ever known."

Maria thought the doctor's stammer added to the charm of his conversation by making his wit and humour more effective. She also "liked Mrs. Darwin exceedingly; there was so much heart, and so little constraint or affectation in all she said and did and looked."

They talked about General Bonaparte, and Darwin expressed himself violently on the subject of war, which, he said, nothing on earth could justify. They drove through the lovely Derbyshire scenery and admired what Anna Seward calls the "umbrageous eminences" (meaning wooded hills) of that district. Dances and card-parties were arranged for the younger members of the two families, while Edgeworth and Darwin discussed electricity, oxygen, manure, and such-like exciting topics, with the ingenious philosophers of the neighbourhood. It was all most enjoyable, and it came to an end far too soon. A hundred "good-byes," spoken and waved, and Edgeworth had bidden a last farewell to his friend.

For, indeed, the doctor's health was beginning to alarm his family. He had been suffering from slight attacks of inflammation in his heart and lungs, and had occasionally been forced to spend a day or two in bed. His son Robert urged him to leave off professional work. He answered: "It is a dangerous experiment, and generally ends either in drunkenness or hypochondriacism. Thus I reason, one must do something (so country squires fox-hunt), otherwise one grows weary of life, and becomes a prey to ennui. Therefore one may as well do something advantageous to oneself and friends or to mankind, as employ oneself in cards or other things equally insignificant."

One relaxation he did, however, permit himself: he left off keeping accounts. The result was that when he had to send in a return for income-tax, he experienced a great deal of unnecessary worry. "I have kept no book," he told Robert, "but believed my business to be £1000 a year, and deducted £200 for travelling expenses and chaise hire, and £200 for a livery servant, four horses and a day labourer." The commissioners accepted his estimate.

His dislike and distrust of the politics and politicians of his time increased with the years. "He was," says Miss Seward, "a far-sighted politician, and foresaw and foretold the individual and ultimate mischief of every pernicious measure of the late Cabinet. . . . On occasions and subjects which he considered trivial, he professed to indulge human prejudice; but whenever by mock assent he extended that indulgence, a slight satiric laugh and a gay disdain lurking in his eye counteracted the assumed coincidence. On circumstances which touched him nearly, he acted steadily upon his own principles. And there were subjects out of himself on which he was always seriously and earnestly ingenuous. Politics was one. He hated war, and thought the motives few indeed which could vindicate its homicide. . . . That of forcing America into internal, unrepresented taxation, and of interfering, through jealousy of her principles, with the internal government of France, he utterly disapproved. The event of both these contests accomplished his prophecies and justified his disapprobation." Perhaps it is as well that no one recorded his opinions when, in 1783, the managers of the Society for the Propagation of the Gospel absolutely declined, after a full discussion, to give Christian instruction to their slaves in Barbadoes. . . .

In spite of his illnesses, his energy continued unabated. He rose early every morning, and had his papers so arranged that if he awoke in the night he was able to get up and continue his work for a time, until he felt sleepy. Yet his youngest son tells us that " he suffered much from a sense of fatigue." It is not surprising that he showed little sympathy with his second son, Erasmus, who bought a house just outside Derby, where he intended to retire from business at the age of forty. In a letter to Robert, the doctor said: " Your brother is going to sleep away the remainder of his life."

Six weeks after the purchase of this house, Erasmus junior committed suicide, and people thought the doctor heartless because he was seen walking about the streets of Derby the day after the funeral " with a serene countenance and his usual cheerfulness of address." But then, as Anna says, he always censured " the folly of suffering our imagination to dwell on past and irretrievable misfortunes, and of indulging fruitless grief. . . . He disdained, from deference to what he termed the prejudices of mankind, to display the outward semblance of unavailing sorrow, since he thought it wisdom to combat its reality." His son Robert backs this up: " He never would allow any common acquaintance to converse with him upon any subject that he felt poignantly. . . . It was his maxim that in order to feel cheerful you must appear to be so."

The doctor himself took over the house, known as Breadsall Priory, which his son had bought. He soon began to improve the place, and he was busy planning out another botanic garden in the grounds, when in the spring of 1801 he had a dangerous illness. Though not in the best of health, he had gone to Derby at the urgent summons of a patient, had caught a severe cold, and the usual complications had set in. He was prostrated with pain about the heart and chest, and a high fever. He bled himself copiously and at length recovered, but his system was irreparably weakened and he began to feel and show his age.

A year later, on 10 April, 1802, he had another attack of inflammation, accompanied by a shivering fit. His surgeon, Mr. Hadley, the husband of one of his natural daughters, bled him freely, taking from him twenty-five ounces of blood in the course of the day. In three days he had quite recovered and said he felt as well as he had done for years. Friends called to inquire after him, and one of them took the opportunity of ascertaining his views on the hereafter. The doctor remarked that it was natural to extend our wishes and views beyond the present scene, and that it was right to pursue such measures as are likely to secure our happiness in another world—"but," he concluded, "let us not hear anything about hell!"

He spent most of Saturday, 16 April, talking and playing in the garden with his children, who were home for their Easter holidays. In the evening, as he was strolling about the grounds with his wife and a lady of his own age, the latter observed that he would have sufficient employment for ten years in perfecting his plans for improving the place.

"You, madam," replied the doctor, "have as good a prospect as anybody I know of your age of living ten years—I have not."

His wife laughed at him and remarked on his present good health, his strength, and spirits.

"I always appear particularly well immediately before I become ill," he said.

Later he sat with his family, talking cheerfully about everything in his usual manner. He rose at six the following morning, went to his library, and began a letter to Edgeworth:

PRIORY, NEAR DERBY,

April 17, 1802.

Dear Edgeworth,

I am glad to find that you still amuse yourself with mechanism, in spite of the troubles of Ireland.

The *use* of turning aside, or downwards, the claw of a table,

I don't see ; as it must then be reared against a wall, for it will not stand alone. If the use be for carriage, the feet may shut up, like the usual brass feet of a reflecting telescope.

We have all been now removed from Derby about a fort-night, to the Priory, and all of us like our change of situation. We have a pleasant house, a good garden, ponds full of fish, and a pleasing valley somewhat like Shenstone's—deep, um-brageous, and with a talkative stream running down it. Our house is near the top of the valley, well screened by hills from the east, and north, and open to the south, where, at four miles distance, we see Derby tower.

Four or more strong springs rise near the house, and have formed the valley, which, like that of Petrarch, may be called *Val chiusa*, as it begins, or is shut, at the situation of the house. I hope you like the description, and hope further that yourself and any part of your family will sometime do us the pleasure of a visit.

Pray tell the authoress that the water-nymphs of our valley will be able to assist her next novel.

My bookseller, Mr. Johnson, will not begin to print *The Temple of Nature* till the price of paper is fixed by Parliament. I suppose the present duty is paid. . . .

At this point the doctor suddenly remembered some instructions he had given one of his servants to ensure the comfort of his horses in their new quarters, his entire establishment having only recently been moved from Derby to Breadsall Priory. He laid down his pen, rang the bell, and asked whether his orders had been carried out. They had not. Few things annoyed him more than inattention to the needs of animals, and he fell into a violent fit of passion. This brought on a cold shivering fit, which increased and was attended with thirst. He went into the kitchen, and while warming himself before the fire drank a considerable quantity of butter-milk. He noticed one of his old servants churning, and asked her why she was doing it on a Sunday morning. She answered that she had always done so, as he liked to have fresh butter every morning.

"Yes, I do," said Darwin, "but never again churn on a Sunday!"

He then returned to the library, where a fire had been lit, and, still feeling ill, lay down on the sofa. At eight o'clock he rang the bell. When the servant came, he told her he was feeling cold and sick, and asked her to send into Derby for Mr. Hadley. She suggested calling Mrs. Darwin, but he wouldn't hear of it. He looked so ill that the servant disobeyed him and went to fetch her mistress.

Mrs. Darwin came, and helped him from the sofa to an arm-chair. At his request the window was closed. His wife was in great distress, but he soothed her, telling her he was in no pain. For a little while they talked together. Then, just before nine o'clock, while Mr. Hadley was hurrying along the road from Derby to the Priory, the doctor became faint, gave a deep sigh, and passed beyond the reach of physic. . . .

BIBLIOGRAPHY

I wish to thank the Rev. Darwin Wilmot for his loan of Erasmus Darwin's Commonplace Book, and for his most generous permission to make what use of it I liked. It has been invaluable.

My cousin, Mrs. Lucy Studdy, gave me much verbal information, and lent me several letters of interest. She also allowed me to read the autobiography of her mother, Mrs. Wheler, Darwin's granddaughter, which has never been published. Mrs. Studdy died before I began my book.

Lastly, I must record my gratitude to my mother, who lent me many family books, papers, and photographs, obtained others for me that were indispensable to my work, and encouraged me in countless ways.

My chief sources of information about Erasmus Darwin have been :

Charles Darwin's " Memoir " of his grandfather, followed by a translation of Ernst Krause's " Erasmus Darwin," 1879. (An excellent biographical essay.)

"Memoirs of the Life of Dr. Darwin," by Anna Seward, 1804. (Over half of this book is devoted to criticism of the doctor's works. All of it is entertaining, though not in the way the authoress meant it to be.)

" Letters of Anna Seward," 6 vols., 1811. (A sheer joy ; but not intended as such by the writer.)

"Memoirs of Richard Lovell Edgeworth," begun by himself and concluded by his daughter, Maria Edgeworth, 3rd edn., 1844. (One of the most readable autobiographies in the language.)

" Sketch of the Life of James Keir, Esq., F.R.S.," printed for private circulation, 1860. (Dull, but contains valuable material.)

" Life of Mary Anne Schimmelpenninck," 2 vols., 1858. (Vol. I contains Mary Anne's autobiography. All the Darwin bits are first-rate. The rest of the book would only amuse an agnostic.)

" The Life of Josiah Wedgwood," by Eliza Meteyard, 2 vols., 1865. (A typically Victorian compilation. Interesting to lovers of ceramic art ; heavy for anyone else.)

"Erasmus Darwin," a Lecture by John Dowson, A.M., M.D., 1861. (Slight, but good.)

Samuel Butler's " Unconscious Memory " and " Evolution : New and Old," are of course familiar to all students of Erasmus Darwin's philosophy ; and, in addition to the foregoing list, I have quoted or obtained information from the following :

" Account of Life and Writings of Thomas Day," by James Keir, 1791. (Official, discreet, and therefore dull.)

" A Memoir of Thomas Day," etc., by J. Blackman, 1862. (Contains several phrases worthy of immortality—e.g. " prattling inmates.")

" An Authentic Account of the Riots in Birmingham," etc., 1791.

" The Life of William Hutton ; including a particular account of the Riots at Birmingham in 1791," etc., by himself, 1816.

" The Poetical Works of Anna Seward, with Extracts from her Literary Correspondence," edited, with a biographical preface, by Sir Walter Scott, 3 vols., 1810. (The extracts are good, but the editor omitted the most delectable passages. Anna's style seems to have had a cramping effect on Sir Walter's sense of humour.)

" A Swan and her Friends," by E. V. Lucas, 1907. (By

introducing the present biographer of Doctor Darwin to Miss Seward, this work places him under an obligation that praise cannot repay.)

" Familiar Letters of Sir Walter Scott" 1894.

" The Monastery," by Sir Walter Scott. (Scott's letter to ' Captain Clutterbuck ' contains his famous passage on James Watt.)

" Life of James Watt, with selections from his correspondence," by J. P. Muirhead, 1858.

" Correspondence of J. Watt," edited by J. P. Muirhead, 1846.

" Lives of Boulton and Watt," by Samuel Smiles, 1865.

" Memoirs and Correspondence of Joseph Priestley," edited by J. T. Rutt, 2 vols., 1831-2. (Nothing but a glance through the files of the British Museum could give the least idea of Priestley's multifarious interests and activities. The list of his works—comprising Histories, Sermons, Inquiries, Remarks, Appeals, Thoughts, Observations, Tracts, Addresses, Discourses, Lectures, Considerations, Essays, Epistles, Outlines, Defences, Introductions, Examinations, Views and Reviews— is enough to make a biographer's head swim or his heart sink. Priestley's letters alone, to private and public persons, on every subject under, above, and around the sun, occupy several volumes. At one moment he addresses an Antipædobaptist on the subject of baptism, at another he dresses down Burke on the subject of the French Revolution. Truly an astonishing creature, who managed to combine an exhaustless interest in the Scriptures with a limitless interest in science. Excepting only Darwin, who never could understand how anyone concerned with the miracle of oxygen could also be concerned over the miracles of Christ, Priestley was quite the most accomplished and versatile member of the Lunar Society.)

" Experiments on the Generation of Air from Water," by Joseph Priestley, 1793. (Dedication to the Members of the Lunar Society.)

" Life of Sir Humphry Davy," by J. Davy, 1839.

" Doctor Johnson and Mrs. Thrale," by A. M. Broadley, 1909. (Mrs. Thrale's Journal of a Tour with Dr. Johnson is printed in this work.)

" The Letters of Horace Walpole," edited by Mrs. Paget Toynbee, Vols. XIV and XV, 1905.

" The Private Correspondence of David Garrick," etc., 2 vols., 1831-2.

" The Life, Letters and Journals of Lord Byron," by T. Moore, 1860.

" The Life, Letters and Labours of Francis Galton," by Karl Pearson, Vol. I, 1914.

" A Memoir of Maria Edgeworth, with selections from her letters," by Mrs. F. A. Edgeworth, 3 vols., privately printed, 1867.

" Literary and Miscellaneous Memoirs," by J. Cradock, 4 vols., 1828. (Vol. I contains the author's reminiscences.)

" Journals and Correspondence of Dr. Whalley," edited by Hill Wickham, 1863. (This work, according to the Dictionary of National Biography, is " burdened with huge epistles from Miss Seward." Readers of *Doctor Darwin* will not need to be told that Miss Seward's letters lighten the burden of the rest of Whalley's correspondence.)

Boswell's *Life of Johnson*, edited by George Birkbeck Hill, D.C.L., vol. V, 1887.

The Poetical Works of William Cowper, edited by H. S. Milford, M.A., 1911.

" Monthly Magazine," June and September, 1802.

" To the Friends of the Monthly Meeting at Birmingham," by Samuel Galton, 1795. (A letter defending his occupation of manufacturing arms.)

Birmingham and Midland Institute—Archæological Section —Transactions, etc., for the year 1889. " The Lunar Society," by Henry Carrington Bolton, Ph.D. (New York), pp. 79-94.

" Transactions of the Historic Society of Lancashire and Cheshire," Vol. VII, 1855. (An article by J. F. Marsh, Esq. " On some correspondence of Dr. Priestley, preserved in the Warrington Museum and Library.")

Dictionary of National Biography.

Dr. Darwin wrote a large number of essays and poems for the journals of his day. My quotations have been taken from his Commonplace Book and his more important works:

The Botanic Garden, a poem in two parts with philosophical notes: Part I, The Economy of Vegetation, 1791; Part II, The Loves of the Plants, 1789.

Phytologia, or the Philosophy of Agriculture and Gardening— with the theory of draining morasses, and an improved construction of the drill plough, 1800.

A Plan for the Conduct of Female Education in Boarding Schools, Derby, 1797.

The Temple of Nature, or the Origin of Society. A poem with philosophical notes, 1803.

Zoonomia, or the Laws of Organic Life, 3rd edition, 4 vols., 1801.

APPENDIX A

From private letters of the period, from memoirs and articles, the following list of members of the Lunar Society has been compiled. There were, possibly, other members, but these may be taken as " official " :

Dr. Erasmus Darwin, F.R.S. (1731–1802).

Captain James Keir (1735–1820).

Thomas Day (1748–89).

Richard Lovell Edgeworth, F.R.S. (1744–1817).

Matthew Boulton, F.R.S. (1728–1809).

James Watt, F.R.S. (1736–1819).

Rev. Dr. Joseph Priestley, F.R.S. (1733–1804).

Dr. William Small (1734–75). Dr. Small held the professorship of mathematics and natural philosophy in William and Mary College, Virginia, for some years before he returned to England and settled in Birmingham.

Dr. William Withering, F.R.S. (1741–99).

John Whitehurst, F.R.S. (1713–88).

Samuel Galton, F.R.S. (1753–1832).

Samuel Tertius Galton, son of the foregoing (1783–1844).

John Baskerville (1706–75). Inventor of superior type and printing, and publisher of standard works.

William Murdock (1754–1839). Mechanical engineer. Superintendent of the works of Boulton and Watt. Inventor of coal-gas lighting, of many improvements in steam machinery, and of the first locomotive road-engine.

Rev. R. A. Johnson, F.R.S. (of Kenilworth).

Dr. Stoke, a Birmingham physician.

Each member was allowed to bring a friend with him to the meetings, and in this way many of the leading men of the day were entertained as guests. Also the society sometimes held " Meetings Extraordinary " in honour of famous foreign scientists. Among the guests known to have been entertained by the " Lunatics " were the following :

Josiah Wedgwood, F.R.S. (1730-95). A constant guest.

Sir Joseph Banks, F.R.S. (1743-1820). Botanist and explorer. President of the Royal Society.

Sir William Herschell, F.R.S. (1738-1822). The leading astronomer of the age.

John Smeaton (1724-92). Civil engineer. Builder of Eddystone Lighthouse.

Dr. Samuel Parr (1747-1825). Eminent scholar and critic.

Rev. Hugh Blair, D.D. (1718-1800). Author of *Lectures on Rhetoric*. Professor in the University of Edinburgh.

Adam Afzelius (1750-1837). Swedish botanist.

Dr. Daniel C. Solander, F.R.S. (1736-82). Swedish naturalist and physician. Assistant librarian at the British Museum ; later, Keeper of the Natural History Department at the British Museum. Secretary and librarian to Sir Joseph Banks, accompanying him on Captain Cook's expedition to Australia, and later going with him to Iceland.

Jean Andre de Luc (1727-1817). Swiss natural philosopher and geologist.

Dr. Pieter Camper, F.R.S. (1722-89). Dutch naturalist and anatomist.

De la Metherie. A famous French chemist.

Rev. Joseph Berington (1746-1827). A somewhat unorthodox Roman Catholic priest of Oscott, a small village seven miles from Birmingham. An impressive personality, and author of several historical works.

Mr. Collins. An American "rebel."

Dr. Henry Moyes, of Edinburgh. Lecturer on chemistry and natural philosophy. Was blinded by smallpox, in infancy ; though, according to Priestley in a letter to Sir Joseph Banks, " superior to most who see." Very argumentative, which pleased Priestley, but made Watt peevish.

William Bewley (*d.* 1783). A surgeon and apothecary of Norfolk. Author of letters on the chemistry of gases and much scientific and literary criticism. A friend of Priestley, and a great friend of Dr. Burney, in whose house in St. Martin's Street he died.

John Wilkinson. An ironmaster. Priestley's brother-in-law.

M. Robinson Boulton, son of Matthew.

APPENDIX B

Darwin's habits as a doctor were as unconventional as his prescriptions. On arrival at a patient's house he usually enjoyed a square meal before going upstairs to the bedroom. This freshened him up after the journey and had a reassuring effect on the anxious relatives of the sick person. Once he was called in to see a surgeon, James Cade, of Spondon, near Derby, who, though seriously ill and unable to speak, was quite conscious, and heard the apothecary ask the doctor, before the latter sat down to dinner, whether he had better bleed the patient again. "Yes", said Darwin, "bleed him again; he may as well die of exhaustion as fever." Cade recovered, probably from shock.

His fondness for food must have appealed to his patients more than his hostility to drink. It is recorded that he drove with one of his sons from Derby to Leicester in order to buy a Stilton cheese. On the way home they picked at the cheese with their fingers. All but a little rind was eaten before they reached Derby.

Believing that human beings could extend their lives considerably, it occurred to him that one way of delaying old age was to take "the warm bath for half an hour twice a week", and he pictured the rejuvenation of an ancient by some such means:

> Pleas'd on the boiling wave old Aeson swims,
> And feels new vigour stretch his swelling limbs;
> Through his thrill'd nerves forgotten ardours dart,
> And warmer eddies circle round his heart;
> With softer fires his kindling eye-balls glow,
> And darker tresses wanton round his brow.

Throughout the Midlands Darwin's carriage was instantly recognisable because one of his horses was always white, whereas other people who drove a pair made a point of matching them.

INDEX

Abridge, 75
Adam, the Sin of, 121
Address to the Inhabitants of Birmingham, Priestley's, 128
Aesculapian Society, 148
Akenside, Mark, 166, 204
America, 78, 122, 125, 157, 220
American War of Independence, 123
Anningley, 77
Anti-Jacobin, The, 208
Appeal, Priestley's, 128
Arabian Nights, The, 217
Archimedes, 105
Aris's Birmingham Gazette, 123
Ashbourne, 154
Aston, 180
Avignon, 59

Babylon, 51
Bacchus, 5
Ballet of Medea, 205
Banks, Sir Joseph, 106
Barberini vase, the, 215
Barclay, Lucy (Mrs. Samuel Galton), 96, 128
Bastille, the, 88
Bath, 67, 92, 170, 172
Beacon Street (Lichfield), 14
Bear Hill (near Wargrave), 50-1
Beau-Desert, 114
Beaumont, Francis, 21
Ben Nevis, 192
Bentley, Thomas, 82, 86-9, 93-5, 108-9
Berkeley, Bishop of Cloyne, 140
Berkshire, 50
Bible, the, 51, 101, 121
Bicknel, Mr., 58, 61, 72-3
Bignor, the "Swan" of, 156

Birmingham, 45-7, 90-1, 99, 108, 112-14, 122-3, 126-9, 152
Birmingham and Staffordshire Chronicle, 124
Birmingham Riots, the, 122-30
Blackman, J., 51, 58, 79
Bonaparte, General, 105, 218
Boothby, Sir Brooke, 36, 49, 218
Bordesley Hall, 126
Botanic Garden, The, 5, 115, 142, 187, 189-91, 200, 204-10
Boulton, Matthew, agrees to buy Darwin's talking-machine, 30; is introduced to Edgeworth, 45; his works at Soho, 46, 108; and partnership with Watt, 46, 89, 109, 113-14; his optimistic nature, 46, 119; his affection for Watt, 46-7; shows Edgeworth over Soho, 47; friendship with Dr. Small, 69; friendship with Watt and Darwin, 81-2; Keir manages his works, 91; member of the Lunar Society, 97; writes to Keir, 103; his appearance, 108; in competition with Wedgwood, 108-9; his ambitious designs, 109; his exaggerations, 109; his great qualities, 110; produces new copper coinage, 110; and wins tribute from Darwin, 110; Lunar Society meetings at his house, 110; receives letter from Darwin, 111; compared with Watt, 111; mentioned in *The Botanic Garden*, 115; attitude during Birmingham Riots, 125; Darwin asks him to make a vase, 164; he turns down Darwin's steam-engine, 210; and receives the doctor's congratulations, 210

INDEX

INDEX

INDEX

INDEX

INDEX

INDEX

INDEX

INDEX

INDEX